Maral Esekeshova
Elmira Kochkorbaeva
Nuria Manapova

Ethnopedagogy

Maral Esekeshova
Elmira Kochkorbaeva
Nuria Manapova

Ethnopedagogy

ScienciaScripts

Imprint

Cover image: www.ingimage.com

This book is a translation from the original published under ISBN 978-613-3-99584-0.

Publisher:
Sciencia Scripts
is a trademark of
Dodo Books Indian Ocean Ltd. and OmniScriptum S.R.L publishing group

120 High Road, East Finchley, London, N2 9ED, United Kingdom
Str. Armeneasca 28/1, office 1, Chisinau MD-2012, Republic of Moldova, Europe
Printed at: see last page
ISBN: 978-620-8-07969-7

CONTENTS.

Preface

As early as the middle of the last century, I. V. Kireyevsky (1806-1856) wrote: "It is as impossible to destroy the peculiarity of people's mental life as it is impossible to destroy their history. It is as easy to replace with literary notions the fundamental beliefs of the people as it is to change the bones of a developing organism by abstract thought. However, if we could allow for a moment that this proposal could, in fact, be realized, then in this case the only result of it would be not in education and enlightenment, but in the destruction of the people themselves. For what is a people if not a set of beliefs, more or less developed in its morals, in its customs, in its language, in its notions of heart and mind, in its religious social and personal relations - in a word, in the entirety of its life".

These words are more relevant than ever at present, the time of "massive attack" on the culture, history and language of all nations, large and small, without exception. The task of teachers is to build a teaching and educational process, the purpose of which is the formation of national consciousness, the development of a child's system of universal values, understanding of the role of their nation, ethnos in the world historical process.

Therefore, the proposed textbook is designed to help students studying the course "Ethnopedagogy" in solving the following problems: familiarizing students with the basic ideas and concepts of ethnocultural education in the Republic of Kazakhstan, as well as with theories and concepts of ethnopedagogy; formation of students' holistic view of folk pedagogy; equipping students with knowledge about the goals, means and methods of folk education; formation of skills to plan extracurricular ethnopedagogical work; formation of students' pedagogical skills:

For each topic of this textbook, a list of basic and additional literature is offered.

Thus, this textbook is structured in such a way that the student can acquire the necessary ethnopedagogical skills in a consistent, digestible manner and in accordance with the curriculum.

1 Subject and objectives of ethnopedagogy

Basic Concepts

Folk pedagogy is a system of family and public education based on the national historical peculiarities of a particular nation, its traditions, customs, faith, and reflecting its mentality, psychological makeup and emotionally aesthetic predilections.

Ethnopedagogy is a science, the subject of study of which is folk pedagogy as a traditional practice of upbringing and education, historically developed by various ethnic groups.

Ethnos is a historically formed community of people united by the unity of language, culture, history and territory of habitation;

People - a class or social stratum (consisting mainly of the working masses), a historically formed community of people united by the unity of language, culture, history and territory of habitation;

Upbringing is a specially organized, purposeful and controlled impact of the collective, educators on the educated person with the aim of forming the given qualities in him/her, carried out in educational institutions and covering the whole educational process.

1.1 Ethnopedagogy as a science. Object, subject and tasks.

The term "ethnopedagogy" was first used in pedagogical literature by G.N. Volkov, who defined it as a science "about the experience of the masses in educating the younger generation, about their pedagogical views, the science of the pedagogy of everyday life, the pedagogy of the family, clan, tribe, nationality and nation. K.D. Ushinsky claimed that folk wisdom is so original in terms of the power of observation, precision of thought, ideological content "that no one is able to compete with the pedagogical genius of the people". Every nation is rich in its centuries-old culture.

Ethnopedagogy is a branch of pedagogical science that studies folk education, pedagogy in different ethnic groups. This field of knowledge is directly related to the traditional culture of upbringing, folklore, everyday pedagogy. It is closely connected with general, social pedagogy, psychology, ethnopsychology, archeology, folkloristics and widely uses data from all social and humanitarian sciences.

The subject of ethnopedagogy is the pedagogical culture of a clan, tribe, nationality, nation. National features of character are the result of ethnic upbringing and the influence of the appropriate environment, so the study of traditional pedagogical culture of sub-ethnic formations (Pomors, Siberians, etc.) is of particular relevance. In ethnopedagogy the object of study belongs to the field of pedagogy proper. The method can be partially borrowed from ethnology, ethnography, anthropology and sociology, but it should be filled with pedagogical content and applied together with purely pedagogical methods. The above is also true for the ethnopedagogical thesaurus: the main concepts are pedagogical, while ethnological and anthropological terms play an auxiliary role.

Objectives of ethnopedagogy:

Formation of national self-awareness, reproduction of ethnic culture

- moral education
- Education of national dignity as a foundation for moral improvement of personality
- mental, labor, physical education

Formation of a perfect human being is the main goal of folk pedagogy.

In the scientific study of folk pedagogy, as indicated above, an important place is given to the historical approach to it. Ethnopedagogy can objectively illuminate pedagogical phenomena only reflecting a certain level of pedagogical knowledge, the historical stage in the spiritual progress of the people, on which the pedagogical science emerged and developed. For many centuries, the people formed the values that gave rise to most of the achievements of modern life. Knowledge of historical and cultural acquisitions of ancestors is necessary not only to comprehend, but also to use the best traditions in the pedagogical practice of today. Ignoring the principle of historicism leads to the separation of the future from the past, to the violation of the historical chain, to the destruction of the natural unity of generations. Ethnopedagogy is also a sphere of historical and pedagogical science, which studies traditional and everyday culture - customs, symbols, traditions, folklore, crafts in different historical periods of development of the state and nation.

1.2 Methods of ethnopedagogical research.

Methods of scientific ethnopedagogical research.

1) on a theoretical level:

- Historical and pedagogical analysis and synthesis (determination of the goals, subject and tasks of the research, development of pedagogical ideas and educational practice of the people in different periods of its ethnogenesis;
- identifying the origins and main directions of the genesis of ethnopedagogy);
- comparison and generalization (processing and ethnopedagogical interpretation of bibliographic indexes, historiographic, ethnographic and folklore publications, archaeological materials);
- historical-structural (with the help of which the acquired historical-pedagogical knowledge is structured and correlated with specific periods and dominant ideas);
- constructive-genetic (consideration of the transformation of historical and pedagogical knowledge during XIII-XX centuries);
- axiological (consists in the correlation between the objects under study and certain values, thanks to which the selection of objects and their evaluation is carried out);

- Personalistic-biographical (used to analyze pedagogical literature on pedagogical personalities);
- predictive (modeling, method of expert evaluations);
- diagnostic (conversations, interviews, "memories in memories");
- Observational (observations in different family settings),
- people, study of labor results).

Literature

1 Ebshova Z. Ethnopedagogy: oku K¥raly. Almaty: Kazak Elem Tshler University 1997. - 230 б.

2 Volkov G.I. Ethnopedagogy. - Cheboksary, 1974. - 376 c.

3 Kazakh ethnopedagogy / Compiled by. C. Kaliev. - Almaty, 1996. - 22 c.

4 Kozhakhmetova K.J. Kazakh ethnopedagogy: methodology, theory, practice. Almaty: Gylym, 1998. - 316 c.

5 Kozhakhmctova K.J. Mcktcptsh ulgtyk terbiye zhyiyesi: theory and practice. - Almaty, 1997. - 142 б.

2 Methodological foundations of ethnopedagogy

Basic Concepts

Methodology is the doctrine of methods of scientific cognition and transformation of the world; the doctrine of principles, forms and ways of building research activities.

Methodology of pedagogy is the doctrine of principles, methods, forms and procedures of cognition and transformation of pedagogical reality.

Ethnosociology is a scientific discipline developed at the intersection of sociology and ethnography. Ethnosociology aims to reveal the ethnic diversity of social processes and, at the same time, the social conditionality and social diversity of functioning of ethnic traits of culture and everyday life in their broad sense.

Ethnopsychology is a branch of social psychology that studies the peculiarities of mental makeup and behavior of people due to their nationality or ethnicity.

Mentality is a model of the world, i.e., a person's ideas about the surrounding reality, himself, his relations with this reality and people (Leontiev AN.).

Ethnic mentality is a way of thinking peculiar to a given people, a stable isomorphism (constancy, invariance, invariant) inherent to a culture, which is usually not realized and is in this culture as natural and not subject to change under the influence of ideological pressure.

2.1 Methodology of pedagogy as a basis for ethnopedagogy

In terms of component composition, K.J.Kozhakhmetova believes that ethnopedagogy is "an integrative field of knowledge, a component of pedagogical science, formed in the bosom of pedagogy at the junction of ethnophilosophy, ethnopsychology, ethnoculture and ethnography, the subject of which are the features of ethnic education, carried out continuously throughout human life in the family and educational institutions.

More multidimensional is another aspect of pedagogy and ethnopedagogy - procedural, the comparative analysis of which allows us to assert that:

First, unlike official pedagogy, ethnopedagogy does not know collective forms of upbringing and excludes the creation of any children's collectives;

Secondly, the absence of collective forms of upbringing in the form of allocation of children to a special social group outside the family implies the absence of the profession of a teacher among adult members of the community - everyone without exception is a teacher in such a community as the traditional ethnos appears to be;

Thirdly, ethnopedagogy is characterized by the inseparable unity of teaching and education *(t^pm-t^rbiye in Kazakhs),* which is unattainable for artificial educational systems (ethnopedagogy is pedagogy, first of all, family pedagogy);

Fourth, the unity of education in ethnopedagogy is manifested in the absence of total control by adults over children's activities and behavior, while in pedagogy the dyad "education - upbringing" is supplemented by a third component - "control", which implies intentional differentiation of children's and adults' activities and behavior in the form of various restrictions on the forms of children's activity, and which has long ago turned into an end in itself, turning education as a full-fledged socialization into a kind of training;

Fifth, the most effective feature of ethnopedagogy is its connection with life, with the practice of teaching and educating the younger generation; it did not and does not need to care about strengthening the connection with life, for it is life itself; there was no need to introduce and disseminate its achievements among the masses;

Sixth, the "school" of ethnopedagogy has a permanent "lesson schedule", uniform for all regardless of age, in other words, the familiarization of children with the spiritual culture of the ethnos is carried out continuously.

Without pursuing the purpose of a thorough polemic with the above statements. We note that they are of scientific interest in terms of identifying differences in the content characteristics of pedagogy and ethnopedagogy. This also does not mean that we are pursuing the goal of opposing the phenomena under discussion. Rather, we are talking about their comparison. As is known, comparison, being one of the components of comparative analysis, ensures the objectivity of interpretation of the compared phenomena.

Thus, based on the above, it can be argued that the commonality of pedagogy and ethnic pedagogy in content terms is expressed in the translation of social experience, in the process of which a person learns social values, the differences are manifested in procedural terms - the ways of transmitting the experience of previous generations to subsequent ones.

In this sense, the methodology of ethnopedagogy is:

1) on the level of private-scientific methodology;

2) by subject content - knowledge of ethnopedagogy knowledge about the subject of ethnopedagogy, the place of ethnopedagogy in the system of pedagogical sciences, its interrelation with other sciences, the goals and objectives of ethnopedagogy;

3) by nature - knowledge of principles, forms and ways of building ethnopedagogical research with reference to known general approaches in pedagogy, as well as in ethnology, ethnophilosophy, ethnopsychology, ethnocultural studies.

Thus, since ethnopedagogy is a constituent, but relatively independent part of pedagogical science and combines ethnology, ethnophilosophy, ethnopsychology, ethnocultural science, its methodological basis should be the main provisions of the above-mentioned sciences with the mandatory priority and guiding role of pedagogy.

2.2 The significance of ethnos theory for ethnopedagogy

"Ethnos" in translation from Greek means "tribe", "people". In science this concept began to be used in the XIX century.

Ethnic (national) phenomena are related to almost all aspects of human life, so they are studied by many disciplines. First of all, it is ethnography, as ethnoses are the main object of its study. In the XX century, this science began to be called "ethnology". Under the name "cultural anthropology" it is a part of modern cultural studies.

Ethnology (ethnography, science of peoples) is a scientific discipline. Both in domestic and world practice, different terms were and are used to designate ethnology. In the past, the term "ethnography" was used more often; nowadays, specialists are more inclined to eliminate differences with the terminology accepted in the world science and prefer the term "ethnology".

Since ethnology studies the vital activity of ethnos, and ethnopedagogy studies ethnic peculiarities of training and education, it is reasonable to dwell in more detail on some theories of ethnos.

L.N. Gumilev's theory of ethnos. According to his concept, ethnos is a stable, naturally formed collective of people, opposing itself to all other similar collectives, which is determined by the feeling of complimentarity, and distinguished by a peculiar stereotype of behavior, which naturally changes in historical time. Every ethnos is internally heterogeneous: within it there may be sub-ethnoses, consortia, and convixia, which may emerge and disintegrate, but the sense of unity of the ethnos as a whole is not lost. These intra-ethnic units are necessary to maintain ethnic unity. (A subethnos is a group ethnographically different from the main mass: consortia are groups of people united by one historical fate (sects, gangs, athels); if consortia are preserved for several generations, they become convixia, i.e. groups of people with the same characteristic life and family ties).

Y.V. Bromley's theory of ethnos. The starting point of his theory is that ethnos combines in different ways, on the one hand, ethnic properties and characteristics, on the other hand, those that are considered as conditions for the formation and existence of ethnic elements proper.

Ethnos receives accordingly a dual nature and two meanings - narrow and broad. Ethnos in the narrow sense was called "ethnikos" (Greek adjective from "ethnos") and included ethnic characteristics, ethnos in the broad sense was called ethno-social organism (ESO) and looked like a combination of ethnic elements and socio-economic factors.

Y.V.Bromley notes that when singling out ethnic groups among other communities of people, it is impossible not to pay attention to the presence of one very obvious external feature of tribes, nationalities, nations and nationalities: each of these entities has its own self-title - its own name, ethnonym. The presence of ethnonym presupposes the existence of self-consciousness in each community. Ethnos represents only that cultural community of people, which realizes itself as such, distinguishing itself from other communities.

System-statistical or component theory of ethnicity.

Ethnos is a historically arisen and evolving complex system with a multicomponent composition (structure):

T component is the territory of settlement of the ethnos.

B - reproduction and demographic structure.

E - production and economic activities.

$ is a system of social relations of institutions.

E - language forms of speech activity.

K - Creating and preserving culture.

C - everyday life (customs, habits, rituals, norms of behavior).

P - psychological aspects of the perception of one's ethnos (self-consciousness).

R - traditional folklore.

P. - A system of personal contact and interaction.

The theory of ethnicity involves analyzing the issues of ethnic psychology in the knowledge of national character, feelings, self-consciousness, ethnic mentality and their purposeful formation.

Ethnopsychology is an interdisciplinary branch of knowledge that studies ethnic features of people's psyche, national character, regularities of formation and functions of national self-consciousness, ethnic stereotypes, etc.

The above definitions show that there are many common points of contact between ethnopsychology and ethnopedagogy: formation of national consciousness, national character, etc.

The following theoretical concepts of ethnopsychology have methodological significance for ethnopedagogy.

Position one. The organization of society, ethnos including, depends on the dynamics of biospheric conditions, and therefore the mechanisms of socio-psychological regulation of man are changing. This obliges educators to creatively rethink historical experience.

Position two. The structure of national psychology, which includes the following components:

- national customs and traditions, national feeling, national character (Sarsenbaev N.);
- national character, awareness of national interests and needs, national self-consciousness (Zhukesh K.);
- national character, national feeling, national taste, national self-consciousness (Elikbaev U.);
- national character, national feeling, national consciousness (Djandildin);

Position three. Scientific concepts related to the phenomenon of mentality:

- mentality is an integral characteristic of people living in a particular culture, which allows us to describe the peculiarity of these people's vision of the surrounding world and explain the specificity of their response to it (Dubov I.G.).

Conclusions: Because ethnopsychology explores the categories of

The main provisions of ethnopsychology are the theoretical and methodological basis of ethnopedagogy.

Literature

1 Anthology of pedagogical thought of Kazakhstan. / Compiled by. K. Zharikbaev, S. Kaliev. - Almaty: Rauan, 1995. - 512 c.

2 Baltabaev M.H. Pedagogical culturology. - Almaty: RIC KAO named after I.Altynsarin, 2000. - 268 c.

3 V.S.Bezrukova. Pedagogy. Projective pedagogy: Textbook for engineering and pedagogical institutes and industrial and pedagogical technical schools. - Ekaterinburg: "Business Book", 1996. - 300 c.

4 Vinogradov G.S. Narodnaya pedagogika. - Irkutstk, 1926. - 293 c.

5 Zhukesh ^. ¥lttyk psychologiologiiynyn, sipaty: Kθmekshi kural. - Almaty: Respubliki baspa kabinetu 1993. - 196 б.

6 Zhumabaev M. Tavdamaly. - Almaty: Ana tsh, 1992. - 106 б.

7 Kenzheakhmetuly S. Kazaktyts Salt, d9stүrleri men edet- Furyptary. - Almaty: Ana ⅛ti, 1994. - 82 б.

8 Kozhabekuly B. Babyrnama. - Almaty: Atatek, 1993. - 273 б.

9 Kozhakhmetova K.J. Kazak khalyk shygarmashy.ajn't otbasynda paidalanu. - Almaty: IPK Alatau, 1997. - 36 б.

3 Ethnopedagogical thought in Kazakhstan

Basic Concepts

Ethnopedagogy is a science, the subject of study of which is folk pedagogy as a traditional practice of upbringing and education, historically developed by various ethnic groups.

Folk pedagogy is a system of education based on the national-historical features of a particular people, its traditions, customs, faith, and reflecting its mentality, psychological makeup and emotional and aesthetic predilections.Folk pedagogy accumulated the main pedagogical ideas of centuries of experience of the people: cooperation in joint life activities, spiritual dedication and charity, the elevation of spiritual needs over "earthly" and much more.

Zhyrau is the most ancient type of poet in Kazakh poetry. The word *"zhyrau"* itself comes from the word *"zhyr" - a* poem, a song, it is first of all a creator. In conditions of nomadic life zhyrau performed many social functions. Many zhyrau, who lived in the XV XVIII centuries, were not only poets, but also tribal leaders, batyr leaders.

3.1.History of development of pedagogical thought of Kazakh people

The history of development of pedagogical thought of Kazakh people can be conditionally divided into **5** stages corresponding to the main periods of social development:

1 **Stage 6-7-15 cc. - folk pedagogy and the origins of scientific pedagogical thought.** The folk pedagogy of Turkic peoples has accumulated rich experience in the upbringing of the younger generation, generalized specific requirements for the education and upbringing of nomadic children. Thus, the requirements for the personality of a jigit are expressed in the winged expression "Sepz kyrly biz syrly" (literal translation "a real jigit has eight qualities and knows how to keep a secret").In the early Middle Ages, mektebs - elementary Muslim schools and madrasas - religious educational institutions of middle and higher type were opened. The pedagogical ideas and activities of Abu Nasir Al-Farabi (870-950), Mahmud Kashgari (XI), Yusuf Balasaguni (XI) and others should be attributed to this period.

2 **stage - the development of Kazakh pedagogical thought from the 15th to the second half of the 19th century.** At this time steppe thinkers - zhyrau entered the public arena. In the period of the Dzungar invasion (XYII - XVIII centuries) pedagogical ideas are represented by the works of zhyrau and akyns: Asan-Kaigy (XY) Bukhar zhyrau (2668 1787). In their works they glorified the **need to** protect the native land from foreigners, proclaimed knowledge as an invaluable wealth, censured greed, pride, laziness and ignorance.

3 **stage - the second half of the 19th century. - Until 1917 the period of intensive development of enlightenment ideas**. In this period a special place belongs to ethnographer, orientalist, educator and traveler Chokan Valikhanov (1835-1864 gg.) Significant contribution to the formation of Kazakh pedagogy Ibrai Altynsarin (1841-1889).The enlightenment activities of Abai Kunanbayev (1845-1904) and the

progressive ideas of Sultanmakhmut Toraigyrov (1893-1920) and Shakrim Kudaiberdiyev (1858-1931) are of significant importance.

Stage 4 - 1917 - 1991 - development of pedagogy as a science in the Soviet period. In the **20s-30s** a significant contribution to the development of pedagogical thought was made by Akhmet Baitursynov (1873-1938) - educator, teacher, organizer of public education; Magzhan Zhumabaev (1889-1935) - author of many scientific publications, textbooks, teaching aids on pedagogy and psychology; Myrzhakyp Dulatov (1885-1935) - public figure, teacher, author of many school textbooks for Kazakh elementary schools. In the **30-40s** of the XX century, a whole pleiad of writers, scientists, and cultural figures were engaged in pedagogical activities and creation of original textbooks for Kazakh schools: Myrzhakyp Dulatov (1885-1935), Magzhan Zhumabaev (1893-1938), Saken Seifullin (1894-1938), Mukhtar Auezov (1897-1961), Sabit Mukanov (1900-1973), Gabit Musrepov (1902-1985) and others.

Since 1991 the 5th stage of development of pedagogy of independent Kazakhstan has begun, when ways of optimization of Kazakhstan education system and integration into the world educational space are sought.

Let us consider the most significant pedagogical ideas of the enlighteners of Central Asia and Kazakhstan.

The outstanding scientist-encyclopedist Abu Nasir Al-Farabi (870950) is the founder of medieval philosophy of the East. There is almost no field of knowledge in which the thinker did not leave profound judgments and ingenious conjectures. Even during his lifetime, he received the title of "Second Teacher" (after Aristotle). And it corresponds to reality, as he solves a number of actual problems of didactics in his scientific and philosophical works. In the pedagogical heritage of al-Farabi are presented the issues of development, creation of means of teaching, education. In this direction, he achieved outstanding successes.

Often in oral teaching, Al-Farabi used methods of heuristic conversation (dialog) and problem-based learning based on solving a controversial problem.

The number of his works, according to researchers of Farabi's heritage, reaches about 200, of which more than 80 works have reached us.

Yusuf Balasaguni. (1019-1085). In his book "Kutadgu bilig" ("Gracious Knowledge"), written in the Turkic language in the form of a poem, the author gives an extensive program for the formation of a well-rounded personality, and he puts education in the first place.

Y.Balasaguni made a great contribution to the development of moral education of the younger generation. His book reveals the ways of upbringing a moral personality. Honesty, truthfulness, kindness, diligence, humanity, loyalty should be brought up in a child. The poet condemns such negative qualities as evil, hypocrisy, laziness, drunkenness, debauchery, calls for moderation and restraint. His treatise contains a number of valuable, practical recommendations on the organization of education not only for children, but also for adults. If you want to be a man, then master knowledge. A man without knowledge is an ignoramus.

Y. Balasagunsky's pedagogical views echo the main provisions of folk pedagogy. The poet, as well as the people, considers family upbringing as the basis for the formation of moral and psychological character of children.

Mahmud Kashgari (1028 or 1029, Barskan, near Lake Issyk Kul - 1101 or 1126, Opal, near Kashgar) was an outstanding Turkic philologist and lexicographer. He was born in the Karakhanid state. He is known for his "Collection of Turkic dialects" *(Divan lugat at-turk*) - a dictionary-guidebook of various Turkic languages. *Mahmud Kashgari* was born in the village of Baryshkhan, near Issyk-Kul. He studied and worked in Kashgar. He left his descendants the work "Divani lugat ta-Turk" ("Dictionary of Turkic dialects"). This work was first published in 1904 by the Hungarian Academy of Sciences. The content and ideological intent of the "Dictionary" go beyond the linguistic. This work is a kind of encyclopedia of the epoch, the main source containing information about different spheres of socio-economic, cultural and scientific life of the peoples of Kazakhstan. Besides philological data, it contains original ideas of ethical and pedagogical and moral and psychological character, in addition to information from the field of anatomy, medicine, veterinary medicine, astronomy, geography, one can find information about other branches of knowledge. The information about the origin of many Turkic-speaking peoples, about the ancestors of present-day Kazakhs - Kipchaks and Kanlys - is of special value. One can also find here the glorification of ardent human emotions, reflections on the meaning of existence, condemnation of greed and cowardice.

The main idea of M.Kashgari's philosophy is the idea of the unity of man and nature, the appeal to the spiritual and moral foundations of man through the comprehension of the native language: "Language is the basis of foundations, the beginning of education and mercy, because a clever word leads to a golden dish, and a bound word cannot be untied with teeth, explanatory words and speeches lead to their cognition, science, knowledge".

Khoja Ahmet Yasawi, *Khoja Ahmet Yassawi* was a Sufi poet. He was born near Sairam settlement. He received initial knowledge from local sheikh Arslan baba, then in Bukhara he listened to a course of lectures on Sufism from Zhusup Hamadani. The beginning of his active preaching activity coincided with the invasion of Kara-Kitai. Later the poet-educator moved to Iasi (now Turkestan). Here he wrote his famous book "Divan-i hikmet" ("The Book of Wisdom"), which was first published in Kazan in 1878. Yassawi's ethical and pedagogical ideas in the light of the philosophical doctrine of Sufism contain the basic norms of ethics of life of poor people ("I seek the hearts of the homeless, the poor, orphans and beggars, and I avoid proud and self-righteous people", "Who cares for the lonely, who cares for the lonely, poor and orphans, he deserves God's approval and help"), calling for patience and asceticism ("Be satisfied with your daily bread"), as well as denouncing the official representatives of Islam ("Whoever ate fat and unclean, praised from the throne for murder, is dust and ashes").

Yassawi adapted his doctrine to the folk traditions of nomads, flexibly combining the canons of Islam with the pantheism of Eastern Sufi doctrines, with elements of shamanism of local Turkic tribes.

One of the main themes of his philosophy is the harmony of the world, the unity of time and space, leading to the unity of man and God, macrocosm and microcosm. Microcosm, according to Yassawi, is the external form of human development, and macrocosm is its inner content ("Man is the whole world, a small sample of the big world"). The basis of his philosophy is the idea of a perfect man, the ascent to the truth, which is possible under the condition of passing four stages: marihat - the law, tarihat - the doctrine of history, mahripat - evening prayer, ahihat - truth. By the example of his own life, the thinker proved the infinite possibilities of the human mind and spirit.

Ahmet Zhuyneki, was born in the village of Zhuynek, near Turkestan. He was blind from birth. His didactic poem "Hikbatul hakayik" ("The Gift of Truth") is characterized by its democratic orientation in comparison with the works of his predecessors. The poem consists of 504 lines. The first section of the poem is devoted to reflections on the benefits of knowledge and harm of ignorance, the second section - poems about careful attitude to language, speech culture, the third section - poems about impermanence and changeability of the world.

The main ideological content of the poem is praise of generosity, simplicity, politeness, pride, as well as condemnation of ignorance, avarice, rudeness, greed: "The wound of a piercing arrow is healable, the wound of an evil tongue does not heal", "Throw away worldly temptations and put on the robes of a righteous man, the most beautiful garment is the garment of justice", "An unmerciful man is like an unfruitful tree: A tree that does not bear fruit is good only for firewood", "A thousand friends are few, a single enemy is many", "He who removes his head for every fault is left without a single living soul in this world", "He who has a good friend becomes a good friend himself".

In the XУ-XУШ centuries thinkers-zhyrau entered the public arena, thanks to the gift of the poetic word they had a certain influence on the masses and gained great authority. Political tolgau (philosophical poems) of Kazakh zhyrau had not only educational and applied, but also ideological and aesthetic value. Asan-Kaigy, Shalkiz-zhyrau, and Zhiyembet zhyrau stood out for their pedagogical orientation. Asan-Kaigy zhyrau dreamed of a happy tomorrow for the Kazakh people. Zhyrau believed that on the Earth, in some corner of it there is a blissful place where there is no oppression and disasters, cold and hunger, people live well and this Earth is called "Zher-yuk" (Promised Land). The works of Shalkiz-zhyrau and Zhiembet-zhyrau evoked interesting thoughts about the personality of a nomad, about the peculiarities of a good and bad man. In their works they glorified the **necessity to** protect the native land from foreigners, proclaimed knowledge as a priceless wealth, censured greed, pride, laziness and ignorance.

Ybrai Altynsarin (1841-1889) is the founder of Kazakh pedagogy. He was an educator-enlightener, poet and prose writer, publicist, creator of the Kazakh alphabet based on the Russian script. He was engaged in organization of educational institutions for training of teachers of elementary school. Altynsarin proposed an original system of schools for the Kazakh population: central (two-class) schools with boarding schools with a six-year term of study, which worked according to the curriculum and programs of district schools; volost (one-class) schools with boarding schools with a four-year term of study; aul mobile schools with a two-year term of study. According to I. Altynsarin, aul schools should work according to the programs of the first two departments of volost schools. He considered education not as an end in itself, but as a means and as a weapon necessary for the youth in the active struggle for the transformation of the social environment. He believed that the school should provide real knowledge that would ensure the achievement of the goal of mental development and moral improvement of the learner's personality. Education was to be conducted in the native language. But I. Altynsarin did not think to limit education of Kazakh people only to elementary schools. He expressed the opinion that it was necessary to create secondary schools and educate Kazakh children in universities.

Chokan Valikhanov (1835 - 1865) was a historian, publicist, linguist, geographer, geographer, musicologist, archaeologist, geographer, traveler, enlightenment democrat. He sharply condemned the situation when the Muslim clergy concentrated public education in their hands, criticized mektebs and madrasahs, where students were forced to learn by heart texts from the Koran without understanding them. Speaking about the nature of education of Kazakhs, Valikhanov presented it as humane and popular, believing that only knowledge and education give a person strength in the struggle for social justice, only knowledge and enlightenment can lead nomads to the path of free development and social progress. The views of Ch. Valikhanov's views on social psychology, in particular, on ethnopsychology, his desire to find out the nature of various ethnopsychological factors speak of his materialistic worldview. The question of psychological features of the peoples of Central Asia, Kazakhstan and East Turkestan Ch. Valikhanov connected with the problems of cultural development and called for the revival of the People's spirit". The scientist understood the manifestation of the peculiarities of folk character in a multidimensional way. Therefore, in a number of his works he scrupulously analyzed the features of everyday life, traditions, customs, language and communication, religion, etc.

Shakarim Kudaiberdiev (1858 - 1931) was a poet- thinker, philosopher, enlightener, composer. Shakarim did not study in special educational institutions, he gained knowledge on his own. He mastered Turkish, Arabic, Persian and Russian languages. He did not limit himself to studying only native and classical oriental poetry, the best samples of Russian and European culture, but carefully studied works on philosophy, psychology, pedagogy, ethics, religion. In his works, the poet urged Kazakh youth to master knowledge, assimilate the achievements of science and use them in practice, to be honest and kind, patient, restrained, refrain from unwise actions, criticized ignorant customs and prejudices of his contemporaries. The scholarly thinker gave a very large place in his work to knowledge and science, educated and scientific people, because he saw in them the hopes associated with the transformation of the inner and outer worlds.

Myrzhakyp Dulatov (18 8 5 - 1935) was a talented journalist and writer. He graduated from Turgai two-class school and pedagogical courses at Kostanay city school, after which he worked as a teacher in aul school and independently studied the works of Russian and Western writers. He left behind a rich spiritual heritage, which reflected the thoughts, experience, traditions of nomadic people, its peculiar aesthetic and ethical national coloring. In 1908 he published collections of poems "Oyan Kazak G" ("Wake up, Kazakh!"), "Masa" (mosquito) and others. Continuing and developing the pedagogical ideas of Kazakh teacher Y.Altynsarin, he paid special attention to scientific and methodological substantiation of the educational process, including new methods, training programs, conducting lessons taking into account the principles of learning theory and didactics. According to M. Dulatov, teaching children is a whole science. Children should be taught to think sequentially, memorize what they read in order and know the content in full.

Magzhan Zhumabaev (1893-1938) - poet, prose writer, teacher and translator. He graduated from the Omsk Teachers' Seminary. Moscow Literary Institute. M. Zhumabaev is one of the first representatives of Kazakhstan and Central Asia, worthily continued the traditions of cultural ties between the East and Europe. He stood at the origins of pedagogical science of Kazakhstan. He is the author of the first textbook on pedagogy, where he derives the basics of pedagogical process from the psychology of learning. His works "Pedagogy" (1922), "Native speech in elementary school" (1923), "Methods of teaching native speech in elementary school" (1925), "Literacy training" (1926), "Primer for adults (1929) and others laid the foundations of Kazakh ethnopedagogy. The textbook on pedagogy made a significant contribution to the creation of pedagogical terminology in the Kazakh language.

M.Zhumabaev singles out education as a separate special section of pedagogical knowledge. Under education the author understands the process of formation and development of a man-citizen, a worthy son of his people working for his benefit.

Mukhtar Auezov (1897-1967).Among the first Kazakh writers who paid attention to the problems of education was the famous Soviet writer M.O. Auezov, who is rightly called a scientist-educator His literary and pedagogical activity was influenced by Ch. Valikhanov, I. Altynsarin, Abay. In 1930 M.Auezov published in Kzyl-Orda the book "Adolescence", which was compiled in accordance with the curriculum of primary classes as a textbook for youth schools. The book should be considered as a scientific work, giving an explanation of the new political phenomena that emerged in the public life of the Kazakh people. M. Auezov's pedagogical works developed the basics of the methodology of independent work of students and self-education. He believes that the teacher should teach children to independently acquire knowledge, work with a book, newspaper, orally and in writing to state their thoughts, make correct conclusions and generalizations. For this purpose it is necessary to apply such teaching methods that would give skills to acquire knowledge independently, to think independently.

Literature

1 Volkov G.I. Ethnopedagogy. - Cheboksary, 1974. - 376 c.

2 Kazakh ethnopedagogy / Compiled by. C. Kaliev. - Almaty, 1996. - 22 c.

3 Kozhakhmetova K.J. Kazakh ethnopedagogy: methodology, theory, practice. Almaty: FbiΛbiM, 1998. - 316 c.

4 Kozhakhmetova K.J. Mekteptsh ulgtyk terbiye zhγyesi: theory and practice. - Almaty, 1997. - 142 б.

5 Ushinsky K.D. About the nationality in public education / Ped.opis: in 6 T./Compiled by S.F.Egorov. S.F.Egorov. - Moscow: Pedagogy, 1988. T. 2. - 527 c.

6 Ethnic pedagogy: A book for reading / Pyatin V.A., Trenev A.M., Alekseeva G.V. et al. - Astrakhan, 1995. - 276 c.

7 Anthology of pedagogical thought of Kazakhstan. K.

Zharikbaev, S. Kaliev. - Almaty: Rauan, 1995. - 512 c.

8 Baltabaev M.H. Pedagogical culturology. - Almaty: RIC KAO named after I.Altynsarin, 2000. - 268 c.

4 Theory of ethnic education

Basic concepts on the topic

Ethnic education is a purposeful process of forming the subject of ethnos. At this stage, in order to understand the essence of the category "ethnos subject" we will limit ourselves to the following formulation: "a comprehensively and harmoniously developed personality", the formation of which is the general goal in pedagogy.

Folk pedagogy (synonym - ethnopedagogy) - a set of knowledge and skills of education, preserved in ethno-cultural traditions, folk ethical and artistic creativity, national-specific sustainable forms of communication and interaction of representatives of different generations with each other and is the most important means of ensuring the unity and continuity of generations, the integrity of the ethnos.

Folk education is a national system of upbringing of a forming integral person with his national self-consciousness, moral, aesthetic, ecological attitude to reality.

4.1 Education as a process of purposeful formation and development of personality

Characterizing education, social and pedagogical sciences first of all emphasize its *social basis.* Human education arises and is carried out only in human society and is deeply dependent on the features and level of development of society. Man is not only a biological being, but also a social one, so his formation depends on the organization of society, on the educational system of the country. The structure and character of the system are in one way or another conditioned by the state, trends in the development of society. The state, authorities express these tendencies and create appropriate education systems, conditions for upbringing.

Psychologists interpret the process of upbringing as a process of interiorization*:* it is the transfer of social, external in relation to the personality knowledge, norms, values into the internal plan of the personality, i.e. the formation of new and new as the development of psychological structures of the personality. On the basis of this, the reverse process becomes possible - *exteriorization* - transfer from the internal plan to the external one, to the activity among people. Thus, in interaction with the environment and the formation of a complex psychological structure of personality takes place.

The ***process of upbringing*** (as pedagogical) - *purposeful, organized activity for the formation and development of a person, characterized by the interaction of educators and pupils and carried out within the pedagogical system (institution).*

In the history of school and pedagogy, classical, traditional principles that are recognized by more or less everyone, confirmed by experience and research have been formed by now, They reflect the most essential regularities of the upbringing process. They form the basis, the system of principles and testify to a certain understanding of the process of education, not only what it is, but also what it should be and what teachers should do to make education more successful. Principles, being a system of leading ideas, requirements to the process of education, not only reflect the laws and are formulated on their basis, but can be the result of pedagogical will, the choice of those and not other principles....

Thus, the principles can be first defined by this or that pedagogical concept, and then in the course of practice and experiments verified, i.e. tested experimentally for truth or adequacy to the real situation in education.

In scientific, methodological and educational pedagogical literature, the reader can see at first glance a variety of principles of education, but if you think about it, in general, a system of principles is given, reflecting the concept of humanistic education. Let us name the main ones:

- education should be aimed at the development of personality, at the formation of creative individuality;
- education should be carried out in accordance with the age and individual characteristics of those being educated;
- Education should take place in the process of the pupils' mastering of culture and in accordance with the peculiarities of the cultural environment and surroundings;
- education requires involving children in active conscious developmental activities;
- education should be closely connected with the life of the surrounding society, with labor, with the experience and life of the pupil;
- Education should be carried out in the collective and with the help of the collective;
- education should be based on the positive aspects of the pupil;
- In education it is required to combine pedagogical guidance with self-activity, independence of pupils.

If we single out the most important among these statements, we will get the following: upbringing should be aimed at the development of creative *personality,* individuality in the process of pupils' *activity* on the mastering of *culture* and on the basis of their age and individual *differences.* We emphasize once again that such a system of principles and the concept of education reflected in them are determined not only by the system of laws of education, but also by a number of the above-mentioned objective factors, as well as by a subjective factor - the will of the pedagogical community or individual teachers.

4.2 A theory of ethnic education.

Throughout history, man has been and remains the object and subject of upbringing. The experience of upbringing accumulated over the centuries, combined with empirical knowledge tested in practice, forms the core of folk pedagogy. However, it should be taken into account that the pedagogical outlook of the people, formed without professional pedagogical training, on the basis of only empirical knowledge, was to some extent spontaneous. The very process of upbringing, everyday pedagogical contact with children was not always conscious. In these conditions, it is striking the ability of the people to select the best, reasonable, corresponding to the folk ideal in the education of a real person. From these positions, folk pedagogy can be considered as a synthesis of national pedagogical experiment. Modern pedagogical theory, enriched by the folk experience of education, gives the opportunity to significantly improve the pedagogical culture of the people, to make sure that the masses play an active role in the development of pedagogical thought as part of the universal culture. Life rules and methods of upbringing are the first laws that a person meets in his life

On the basis of the fact that education in philosophy is defined as the reproduction of social experience in an individual, as the translation of human culture into an individual form of existence, and also, recognizing that any human culture, and the man himself have, first of all, an ethnic origin, it is legitimate to assert that education always has an ethnic origin.

Folk wisdom about education is an expression of centuries of pedagogical culture.

If we make a comparative analysis of the works of great thinkers and folk views on education, we can see their complete unity, mostly in the form of easily remembered aphorisms. The figurative word, performing, on the one hand, a pictorial-expressive, on the other - information-communicative function, served as a link between the admonitions of thinkers and the richest aphorisms of the people. Great pedagogues of different times and peoples in their works developed the ideas of nationality, nature-appropriate education, widely used examples from folk pedagogy as an expression of folk wisdom.

Folk pedagogy, being the predecessor of scientific pedagogy, has some peculiar and characteristic features in the epistemological, historical, logical and structural respects. Analyzing the content and forms of monuments of folk pedagogy, we can identify its distinctive features.

Folk pedagogy was historically formed in ancient times. It has existed for as long as the people themselves have existed.

On this basis, introducing the category of "ethnic education" into scientific circulation, Kozhakhmetova K.Zh., gives her definition: inter-colonial interaction, in the process of which an individual learns the values of his ethnicity.

Thus, ethnic education (to some extent synonymous with the concept of "folk pedagogy", as it is based on empyrean knowledge) is a purposeful process of forming the subject of ethnicity. At this stage, in order to understand the essence of the category "ethnos subject", we will limit ourselves to the following formulation: "a comprehensively and harmoniously developed personality", the formation of which is the general goal of pedagogy.

Based on the last definition of the concept of "ethnic education", it can be argued that its goal is the formation of the subject of ethnicity.

The objectives of ethnic education are:

- to give ideas about the ethnic picture of the world and its integrity;
- to give knowledge of the history, language, culture and territory of the native ethnic group;
- to develop beliefs in the need to preserve, transform and transmit ethno-social values in their unity with universal values;
- to promote the development of skills and abilities to preserve, transform and transmit ethno-social values in their unity with universal values.

The basic principles and ethnic education are:

- the principle of dialectical unity of the ethnic, interethnic and universal;
- the principle of continuity;
- the principle of infinity;
- the principle of cultural appropriateness (taking into account the mental peculiarities of the individual);
- the principle of nature expediency (taking into account the vital features of the biological organism), first of all, the principle of gender and age differentiation;
- the principle of mastering ethno-social roles.

The leading principle of ethnic education is the principle of nature expediency.

The idea of the necessity of nature-based education is found in the works of Democritus, Plato, and Aristotle. The principle of nature-appropriateness of education was first founded and developed by J.A. Kamensky in the 17th century. J.J. Rousseau and I.G. Pestalozzi attached great importance to this principle in their pedagogical systems. Although each of them understood the principle of nature expediency somewhat differently, they were united by the approach to man as a part of nature and, in this connection, by the assertion of the necessity of his education in accordance with the objective laws of human development in nature.

Thus, ethnic education (to some extent synonymous with the concept of "folk pedagogy", since it is based on empirical knowledge) is a purposeful process of forming the subject of ethnicity. At this stage, in order to understand the essence of the category "ethnos subject", we will limit ourselves to the following formulation: "a comprehensively and harmoniously developed personality", the formation of which is the general goal in pedagogy.

In generalized form, ethnic education can be presented in the form of its structural and logical model.

Structural and logical model of ethnic education

System-forming components	Characterization of components
IDEA	ethnic self-preservation

OBJECTIVE	ethnos subject formation
CHALLENGES.	to give knowledge of native language, culture, history, territory; To develop skills and abilities to preserve, transform and transmit ethno-social values in their dialectical unity with universal human values; to form beliefs about the integrity and indivisibility of the ethnic picture of the world; to promote the development of the desire for self-knowledge and cognition of others
PRINCIPLES	the principle of nature expediency (taking into account the vital features of the biological organism); the principle of cultural appropriateness (taking into account the mental peculiarities of the individual); the principle of nationality; the principle of syncretism and infinity; ethno-social-role approach
METHODS	methods of encouragement (blessing, caressing, wishes, gifts, etc.); methods of punishment (affectionate reproach, imaginary indifference, boycott, cursing, etc.); prohibitions the "carrot and stick" method (al-Farabi)
DIRECTIONS	Oral folk art (children's folklore genres); holidays;
	rites, rituals, customs, holidays
RESULT	ethnos actor

Literature

1 θ6iΛ0βa Z. Ethnopedagogy: oku k^raly. Almaty: Kazak Elem TigΛep University 1997. - 230 б.

2 Volkov G.I. Ethnopedagogy. - Cheboksary, 1974. - 376 c.

3 Kazakh ethnopedagogy /Compiled by. S.Kaliev.- Almaty, 1996. - 22 c.

4 Kozhakhmetova K.J. Kazakh ethnopedagogy: methodology, theory, practice. Almaty: Gylym, 1998. - 316 c.

5 Kozhakhmetova K.J. Mekteptsh ulpyk terbiye zhγyesi: theory and practice. - Almaty, 1997. - 142 б.

6 Ushinsky K.D. About the nationality in public education / Ped.opis: in 6 T. /

Comp. C. F. Egorov. - Moscow: Pedagogy, 1988. T. 2. - 527 c.

7 Ethnic pedagogy: A book for reading / Pyatin V.A., Trenev A.M., Alekseeva G.V. et al. - Astrakhan, 1995. - 276 c.

5 Methods and means of ethnic education

Basic concepts on the topic

Kazakh ethnopedagogy is already singular, which was formed due to the originality of ethnic culture, expressed in language, traditions, customs, rituals, religion. At the expense of a peculiar ethnic worldview, formed historically under the influence of environmental conditions, life, economic activity, ethnic psychology of Kazakhs, which finds its expression in his character, national feelings, national consciousness.

Upbringing - purposeful formation of personality in order to prepare it for participation in social and cultural life in accordance with socio-cultural normative models.

Traditions - a set of ideas, rituals, habits and skills of practical and social activities, passed from generation to generation, acting as one of the regulators of social relations.

Educator (educator) - in the general sense - a person who carries out education, in the narrow sense - an official who performs educational functions in an educational institution.

7.1 Means, forms and methods of upbringing in Kazakh ethnopedagogy.

Throughout history, man has been and remains the object and subject of upbringing. The experience of upbringing accumulated over the centuries, combined with empirical knowledge tested in practice, forms the core of folk pedagogy.

Folk pedagogy, being the predecessor of scientific pedagogy, has some peculiar and characteristic features in the epistemological, historical, logical and structural respects. Analyzing the content and forms of monuments of folk pedagogy, we can identify its distinctive features.

Folk pedagogy was historically formed in ancient times. It has existed for as long as the people themselves have existed.

On this basis, introducing the category of "ethnic education" into scientific circulation, Kozhakhmetova K.Zh., gives her definition: inter-colonial interaction, in the process of which an individual learns the values of his ethnicity.

Thus, ethnic education (to some extent synonymous with the concept of "folk pedagogy", as it is based on empirical knowledge) is a purposeful process of forming the subject of ethnicity. At this stage, in order to understand the essence of the category "ethnos subject", we will limit ourselves to the following formulation: "a comprehensively and harmoniously developed personality", the formation of which is the general goal in pedagogy.

The content of ethnic education is the main directions of education, namely: moral and spiritual education, labor education, mental education, physical education, aesthetic education.

The heart of ethnic education is labor education.

Let us now consider the methods of ethnic upbringing. Centuries of experience have allowed the people to develop certain didactic methods and rules of bringing up children.

In everyday practice there are also methods of educational influence on children, such as explanation, teaching, encouragement, approval, persuasion, personal example, demonstration of exercises, hint, rebuke, condemnation, punishment, etc. Explanation and persuasion were used to form in children a positive attitude to work, decent behavior in the family and society. Of particular importance was the demonstration of ways of performing various types of agricultural, craft and household labor (handling tools and implements, cultivating the land - watering, harvesting, caring for livestock, preparing national dishes, weaving, carving, embroidery, etc.). After explanation and demonstration, exercises usually came into force, which were accompanied by the advice: "Exercise your hands, develop a habit of certain work". Listening to the advice of adults, young men and women had to develop the necessary skills and techniques of labor.

Exhortation is the most widespread technique in ethnic pedagogy. In the monuments of old pedagogy there is a code of admonitions of elder to younger, teacher to student, folk sage to youth, father to son.

It is characteristic that folk educators took care to include in their aphorisms various pedagogical categories: admonition, warning, rebuke, even certain pedagogical conditions under which one can expect success in any endeavor. These conditions are usually determined by the word "if". The Cossacks believe ((If a six-year-old returns from a journey, he should be visited by a sixty-year-old". The Karakalpaks on the basis of Chinese wisdom and philosophy advise: "If you sow millet, do not wait for wheat".

A common method of ethnic upbringing is teaching. The people say: "Things are washed with water, a child is brought up by training".

Persuasion as a method of education contains clarification (explanation) and proof, i.e. showing concrete examples, so that the child does not hesitate and does not doubt the reasonableness of certain concepts, actions, deeds, gradually accumulate moral experience and the need to be guided by it.

Encouragement and approval as a method of upbringing were widely used in the practice of ethnic upbringing. A child has always felt the need to evaluate his behavior, play, work. Verbal praise and approval of parents is the first encouragement in the family. Knowing the role of praise as a means of encouragement, people remark: "children and gods love to be where they are praised". Parents usually approve the behavior, educational and labor successes of children with the words "well done", "good", "very good". In this case, the people pedagogically very reasonably established that the words of approval and praise should be said with a smile on the face. If the work is not done at the proper level, parents will say: "Nothing", "Okay, it will do", but without a smile. Children easily understand how their work is appreciated.

Considering the educational power and effectiveness of innuendo, people created their own cautionary tales. As GN. Volkov, "the pedagogical value of innuendo is that they allow you to talk about the shortcomings of a boy's behavior in a harmless tone".

We can safely say that the hint expressed the pedagogical tact of the people, their intuition.

Personal example (especially of parents) is the most radical, the most effective method of ethnic education. The moral character of parents, their labor, social activities, relationships in the family, attitude to people around them, attitude to things, art - all this serves as an example for children and influences the formation of their personality. Folk wisdom says that positive example should be used in upbringing; "If you have a grown-up son, make friendship with a modest person, if you have a grown-up daughter, make friendship with a craftswoman"

The most poetic form of educational influence on children was parental blessing. "Let your home be blessed, live until the wedding of your children," people would say to a person creating a young family.

Ethnic pedagogy did not ignore such methods of upbringing as punishment, censure, prohibition and rebuke; verbal condemnation of bad deeds and rash actions was used more often. Condemnation was accompanied by suggestion to make the child realize his mistakes and eliminate them. Parental rebuke was rarely used, mainly as one of the educational preventive measures.

Oral folk art is a means of ethnic education. Genres of children's folklore occupy a special place here.

Literature

1 Ebshova Z. Ethnopedagogy: oku k^raly. Almaty: Kazak Elem Tshler University 1997. - 230 б.

2 Volkov G.I. Ethnopedagogy. - Cheboksary, 1974. - 376 c.

3 Kazakh ethnopedagogy /Compiled by. C. Kaliev.-Almaty, 1996. - 22 c.

4 Kozhakhmetova K.J. Kazakh ethnopedagogy: methodology, theory, practice. Almaty: Fylym, 1998. - 316 c.

5 Kozhakhmetova K.J. Mekteptsh ulgtyk terbiye zhγyesi: theory and practice. - Almaty, 1997. - 142 б.

6 Ushinsky K.D. About the nationality in public education / Ped.opis: in 6 T. / Comp. C. F. Egorov. - Moscow: Pedagogy, 1988. T. 2. - 527 c.

7 Ethnic pedagogy: A book for reading / Pyatin V.A., Trenev A.M., Alekseeva G.V. et al. - Astrakhan, 1995. - 276 c.

6 Ethnic subject as a goal and result of ethnic education

Basic concepts on the topic:

The **individual** is "a single representative of the human species, a form of biological individual", his mental process takes place at the biological level, the ways of existence are limited to auditory, visual, tactile perception of existence.

Ethnic education is a purposeful process of forming the subject of ethnos.

Parasat (literally - consciousness, reason, intellect, wisdom). This component, forming the cognitive sphere of personality, corresponds to its cognitive, intellectual activity;

^aHaFam (literally, contentment, gratitude, to be able to be thankful for the little one has; but by no means does it mean to be content with little, however, one must not overstep another's "freedom" when accomplishing a goal).

θgiΛeτ (literally - justice, truth: the highest measure of man's relationship with society, with nature, with the world)

Deulet (literally - prosperity, well-being, material wealth; a person's first and foremost wealth is their physical and mental health)

Culture is the basis of the mentality of any society, its peculiar equivalent.

An **ethnos subject** is a person who has cognized his/her nature and ancestral history, actively transforms national culture and is ready to pass on the social experience of his/her ethnos to subsequent generations through the preservation and enrichment of his/her native language.

7.1 The concept of the subject of ethnos

An individual is "a single representative of the human race, a form of a biological individual", his mental processes are at the biological level, his ways of existence are limited to auditory, visual, tactile perception of existence. Its main purpose is to fulfill the role of a continuer and multiplier of the population.

A.N. Leontiev, defining the concepts of "individual" and "personality", specifies the field of their intersectionality, expressed in the integrity of both, and divides these concepts on the basis of analyzing the nature of this integrity, when for "individual" it is determined by "genotypic formation", and for "personality" - by a social factor. On this basis, he argues that "personality is a relatively late product of socio-historical and ontogenetic development of man".

As K.K.Platonov states, "the structure of personality has at least four substructures:

- socially conditioned substructure (the properties of this substructure characterize the core of a person's citizenship, and determines the motivation of activity in all spheres of activity);
- individually acquired experience;
- individual characteristics of mental processes;

- biologically (genetically) determined personality traits".

B.G. Ananyev states the same, distinguishing four main interacting sides of personality "biologically conditioned features, features of individual mental processes, experience of personality, socially conditioned qualities of personality". Moreover, he specifies that the social side is dominant in determining the essence of personality. And in this regard, ranking human behavior and activity, he prefers behavior as a "generic characteristic, in relation to which all types of activity have a private meaning".

As B. G. Ananyev notes: "Speaking of man as an individual, about the totality of his individual properties, we can mean both his organism at a certain stage of development and his personality. The relations between organism and personality are treated as two layers, levels of human being, and the organism - as a natural basis, a set of natural prerequisites for the formation of personality, and personality - as a supra-organismal, socially conditioned formation". Among the personal formations B. G. Ananyev refers to the status of a person, i.e. the position in society (economic, political, legal, etc.); social functions performed by a person depending on this position and historical epoch; motivation of his behavior and activity depending on the goals and values that form his inner world; worldview and the totality of relations of a person to the surrounding world (nature, society, labor, other people, himself); character and aptitudes.

The doctrine of the personality of the ancient Kazakh thinker J. Balasaguni is of fundamental importance for us. Balasaguni. The peculiarity of his interpretation of personality lies in the fact that he distinguishes four structural basic components of personality:

Parasat (literally - consciousness, reason, intellect, wisdom). This component, forming the cognitive sphere of personality, corresponds to its cognitive, intellectual activity;

^aHaFam (literally - satisfaction, gratitude, to be able to be grateful for the little you have; but by no means means means to be satisfied with little, however, in achieving the goal one must not overstep someone else's "freedom"). It corresponds to the value-oriented activity of the personality, forming its spiritual and moral sphere;

θgiΛeт (literally, justice, truth: the highest measure of man's relationship with society, with nature, with the world. Let us add that justice in J.A. Komensky is interpreted as follows: not to take someone else's goods, not to steal from others, not to upset others). Forming the socio-normative sphere of personality, it corresponds to its communicative, evaluative-regulative activity;

Deulet (literally - prosperity, well-being, material wealth; the first and main wealth of a person is his physical and mental health). This structural component, forming the psycho-physiological sphere of personality, corresponds to its aesthetic, physical and transformative (practical) activity.

A human being is a dynamic system, becoming a personality, manifesting itself as such in the process of interaction with the environment.

Culture is the basis of the mentality of any society, its peculiar equivalent. Culture is a holistic environment, as D.S. Likhachev figuratively expressed in this regard: "This is a huge holistic phenomenon that makes people inhabiting a certain space, from a simple population - a people, a nation. The concept of culture should include and has always included religion, science, education, moral and moral norms of behavior of people and the state". **The subject of ethnos** is a person who has learned his/her nature and ancestral history, actively transforming the national culture and ready to pass on to subsequent generations the social experience of his/her ethnos through the preservation and enrichment of the native language.

Literature

1 Anthology of pedagogical thought of Kazakhstan. / Compiled by. K. Zharikbaev, S. Kaliev. - Almaty: Rauan, 1995. - 512 c.

2 Baltabaev M.H. Pedagogical culturology. - Almaty: RIC KAO named after I.Altynsarin, 2000. - 268 c.

3 V.S.Bezrukova. Pedagogy. Projective pedagogy: Textbook for engineering and pedagogical institutes and industrial and pedagogical technical schools. - Ekaterinburg: "Business Book", 1996. - 300 c.

4 Vinogradov G.S. Narodnaya pedagogika. - Irkutstk, 1926. - 293 c.

5 Goncharov I. New school of Russia: what to be // Education of schoolchildren. - 1997. - № 2. - C. 36-42.

6 Danilyuk A.Ya. The concept and understanding of the Russian national school // Pedagogy. - 1997. -№ 1 - C. 38-40.

7 Dneprov E.D. Educational reform and national school. // National School: state, problems, prospects / Edited by M. N. Kuzmin. - M. N. KUZMIN, 1995. C. 34-40.

7 The ideal of the perfect person in folk pedagogy

Basic concepts on the topic

Folk pedagogy is a set of accumulated and practice-tested empirical knowledge, skills and abilities, transmitted from generation to generation mainly in oral form as a product of historical and social experience of the masses.

Ideal - in the common sense: a) the highest degree of value or the best, completed state of any phenomenon, b) individually accepted standard (recognized sample) of something, usually concerning personal qualities or abilities; 2) in the strict ethical sense: in theoretical terms - a) the most general, universal and, as a rule, absolute moral representation (of the good and the proper), in normative terms - b) perfection in relations between people or (in the form of a social ideal) such an organization of society, which provides this advice

7.1 The popular ideal of the perfect person.

The folk ideal of the perfect man should be regarded as a summarized, synthetic idea of the goals of folk education. The goal, in turn, is a concentrated, concrete expression of one of the sides of upbringing. The ideal is a universal, broader phenomenon, expressing the most general task of the whole process of personality formation. The ideal shows the ultimate goal of upbringing and self-education of man, gives the highest example to which he should strive.

The moral ideal carries a huge social charge, playing a purifying, calling, mobilizing, inspiring role. When man learned to walk on all fours, Gorky wrote, nature gave him an ideal in the form of a staff. Belinsky highly valued the role of the ideal in human progress, in the ennobling of the individual; at the same time, he attached great importance to art, which, as he believed, forms a "longing for the ideal.

Among the many treasures of folk pedagogical wisdom, one of the main places is occupied by the idea of the perfection of human personality, its ideal, which is a model for imitation. This idea originally - in its most primitive form - emerged in ancient times, although, of course, the "perfect man" in the ideal and reality is much younger than the "reasonable man" (the first arises in the depths of the second and is part of it). Education in a truly human sense became possible only together with the emergence of self-education. From the simplest, isolated, accidental "pedagogical" actions, man went to the increasingly complex pedagogical activity. According to Engels, even at the dawn of mankind "people acquired the ability to perform more and more complex operations, to set themselves higher and higher goals (emphasis mine. - G.V.) and to achieve them. Labor itself became from generation to generation more diverse, more perfect, more multifaceted". Progress in labor led to progress in education, which is inconceivable without self-education: setting goals for oneself is its concrete manifestation. As for the goals of "higher and higher", they testify to the birth of the idea of perfection in the depths of the still primitive forms of education. The variety, perfection and versatility of labor, about which F. Engels wrote, demanded, on the one hand, human perfection and, on the other hand, promoted this perfection.

The formation of the perfect man is the leitmotif of national education. The most convincing and most vivid evidence of the fact that man is "the highest, most perfect and most excellent creation" is his constant and irresistible striving for perfection. The ability to self-perfection is the highest value of human nature, the highest dignity, the whole meaning of so-called self-realization lies in this very ability.

The very concept of perfection has undergone historical evolution along with the progress of mankind. The first glimpses of consciousness of human ancestors are connected with the instinct of self-preservation; from this instinct later grew a conscious concern for health promotion and physical perfection (according to Comenius - about harmony in relation to the body). Labor created man. The aspiration to improve the tools of labor awakened the inner aspiration to self-improvement. Already in the most primitive tools of labor begin to manifest elements of symmetry, generated not only by the desire for convenience, but also for beauty. In the struggle for existence, human ancestors met with the need to coordinate their actions and provide - albeit at first unconsciously - to help each other. The very eternal harmony of nature and the activity of man's relationship with it made it natural to improve individual qualities of human personality. The idea of harmonious perfection of the personality was embedded in the very nature of man and in the nature of his activity. The most primitive tools of labor were at the same time the carriers of the incipient primitive spiritual culture: they stimulated the first glimmers of consciousness, causing tension of the twilight mind of the foreman; not only hands distinguished between the convenience and inconvenience of stone tools, but also eyes began to notice the attractiveness of the convenient, and this selectivity was the beginning of the primitive sense of beauty.

The perfection of the individual turned out to be conditioned by the two greatest acquisitions of the human race - heredity and culture (material and spiritual). In turn, human progress would have been impossible without people's striving for perfection. This perfection itself, generated by labor activity, went in parallel in the sphere of material and spiritual culture, went on in man, outside him and in human communication.

Literature

1 Volkov G.N. Ethnopedagogics. Moscow, 1999.

2 Volkov G.N. Ethnopedagogy. Cheboksary, 1974.

3 Izmailov A.E. Folk pedagogy: pedagogical views of Central Asia and Kazakhstan , M., 1991

4 Kon I.S. Ethnography of childhood //Traditional forms of upbringing of children and adolescents in the peoples of East and Southeast Asia. -M., 1983.

5 Kozlov V.I. Ethnos and culture //SE, №3., 1979.

8 Means of folk pedagogy

Basic concepts on the topic

Proverb - a small form of folk poetry, dressed in a brief, rhythmic utterance, carrying a generalized thought, conclusion, allegorical with didactic bias.

A **riddle** is a metaphorical expression in which one object is depicted by means of another object that has some, even if remote, resemblance to it; on the basis of the above, a person must guess the conceived object. Riddles are found in all peoples, at whatever stage of development they did not stand. A proverb and a riddle differ in that a riddle must be guessed, while a proverb is a teaching.

A folk song is a piece of music whose author is not known; as a rule, the author is the people themselves. Folk songs are passed down from generation to generation. Over time, the people may insert new words and sentences, and the result is a folk song.

A **fairy tale** is one of the genres of folklore or literature. An epic, mostly prose work of a magical nature, usually with a happy ending. As a rule, fairy tales are intended for children.

1 .1 Proverbs. Riddles. Folk songs. Fairy tales

Proverbs. In any proverb there is always a "pedagogical moment" - edification: a proverb is understood as an apt figurative saying of an edifying nature, typifying various phenomena of life and having the form of a complete sentence.

Proverbs satisfied many spiritual needs of workers: cognitive-intellectual (educational), industrial, aesthetic, moral, etc.

Proverbs are not antiquity, not the past, but the living voice of the people: people keep in their memory only what they need today and will need tomorrow. When a proverb speaks of the past, it is evaluated in terms of the present and the future - condemned or approved depending on the extent to which the past, reflected in the aphorism, corresponds to the people's ideals, expectations and aspirations.

A proverb is created by all the people, so it expresses the collective opinion of the people. It contains people's assessment of life, observations of people's mind.

"Children are not taught by beatings, but by a kind word", "Children are punished with shame, not with a thunderbolt and a scourge", "Take pity on your own, and then on strangers! One's own is another's friend"

An important pedagogical meaning has popular opinion about the results of education, these are evaluative judgments about people, about the traits of their personality: "A hot temper is not deceitful", "An evil person is like coal: if it does not burn, it blackens", "A good conscience is the eye of God. A good conscience loves reproof"

Considering labor as a moral factor, people emphasize its psychological significance and note that labor gives a person mental and moral satisfaction: "Without labor, there is no peace", say the Avars; "A friend made it easier for the body, a friend made it easier for the soul", say the Lezgins and Tabasarans; labor is the source of life on earth: "Without labor, there is no life on earth", say the Dargins.

Riddles. Riddles are clever, highly poetic, and many carry a moral message. Accordingly, they influence mental, aesthetic, and moral education. In ancient times they probably fulfilled all these functions more or less equally. But later, mental education became the dominant element in them.

Riddles are designed to develop children's thinking, to teach them to analyze objects and phenomena from different areas of reality, and the presence of a large number of riddles about the same phenomenon allowed to give a comprehensive characteristic of the subject (phenomenon). But the importance of riddles in mental education is not limited to the development of thinking, they also enrich the mind with information about nature and knowledge from various areas of human life. The use of riddles in mental education is valuable because the totality of information about nature and human society is acquired by the child in the process of active thinking activity.

Riddles contribute to the development of the child's memory, his imaginative thinking, quick mental reactions.

A riddle teaches a child to compare the features of different objects, to find common features in them and thus forms the ability to classify objects, to discard their unimportant features. In other words, with the help of a riddle, the foundations of theoretical creative thinking are formed.

A riddle develops a child's observation skills. The more observant the child, the better and faster he guesses riddles. What a marvelous process takes place, for example, in the child's head, when he quickly finds a similarity between a grandfather, wearing a hundred coats, and an onion, or between a maiden sitting in prison with a scythe to the street, and a carrot!

Folk songs

Songs reflect the age-old expectations, aspirations and innermost dreams of the people. Their role in education is enormous, perhaps incomparable to anything else. Songs are unique in the musical and poetic design of the idea ethical, aesthetic, pedagogical. Beauty and goodness in the song appear in unity. Good young men, sung by the people, are not only kind, but also beautiful. Folk songs have absorbed the highest national values, oriented only on the good, on human happiness.

The song is characterized by high poeticization of all aspects of folk life, including the education of the younger generation. The pedagogical value of song is that beautiful singing was taught, and it, in turn, taught beauty and goodness. Song accompanied all events of folk life - labor, holidays, games, funerals, etc. The whole life of people passed in song, which best expressed the ethical and aesthetic essence of the individual. The complete song cycle is the life of a person from birth to death. Songs are sung to a baby in the cradle, who has not yet learned to understand, to an old man in the coffin, who has ceased to feel and understand. Scientists have proven the beneficial role of gentle song in the mental development of the child in the womb. Lullaby songs not only put the baby to sleep, but also caress him, soothe him, bring joy. Italians have wake-up songs to make the baby wake up in a good mood and meet the coming day in joy.

Noteworthy means of educational influence are ***pestushki*** and ***sweets.*** In them, the growing child fully occupies the attention of the adult. Pestushki got its name from the word pestuvatovat - to coddle, carry in his arms. These are short verse refrains, which accompany the movements of the child during pesting. Thus, for example, Chuvash mothers express the wish: "Be big, be big - with each pull up an inch add to your height". But pestushki do not aim the child at physical development, i.e. they are not only the simplest physical exercises accompanied by songs of good wishes.

Nevertheless, teenagers also have their own poetry. These are ***tosses, cursive words, counting, teasing*** in numerous varieties. In counting strictly observed consonance and rhythm, their artistic function - it is in a kind of play with words and rhythm, which are characterized by vivacity and colorfulness. When performing counting songs, children decorate them with a simple melody, and sometimes just use the melody of a well-known children's song.

Many teenage songs praise hard work, courage, bravery, determination, etc.

Songs of adult men and women, songs of parents are even more diverse in genre. These songs are closely connected with the life of the people. ***Ritual and ceremonial songs*** predominate among them. There are even more songs about labor and struggle, songs of social protest. They do not directly raise the problems of education, but educate by melody, thought, feelings, the example of the heroes sung, events from the people's life.

Fairy tales. K.D.Ushinsky called fairy tales of the Russian people the first brilliant attempts of folk pedagogy. Admiring fairy tales as monuments of folk pedagogy, he wrote that no one is able to compete with the pedagogical genius of the people. The same should be said about fairy tales of other nations.

The material for folk tales was the life of the people: their struggle for happiness, beliefs, customs, - and the surrounding nature. In the beliefs of the people was a lot of superstitious and dark. This dark and reactionary - a consequence of the difficult historical past of the workers. Most of the tales reflect the best traits of the people: diligence, giftedness, loyalty in battle and labor, boundless devotion to the people and the motherland.

Fairy tales, being artistic and literary works, were at the same time a field of theoretical generalizations on many branches of knowledge for the workers. They are the treasury of folk pedagogy, moreover, many fairy tales are pedagogical works, i.e. they contain pedagogical ideas.

Fairy tales are an important educational tool, for centuries developed and tested by the people. Life, folk practice of upbringing has convincingly proved the pedagogical value of fairy tales. Children and fairy tales are inseparable, they are created for each other and therefore acquaintance with fairy tales of their own people must necessarily be included in the course of education and upbringing of every child.

Literature

2 Volkov G.N. Ethnopedagogics. Moscow, 1999.

3 Volkov G.N. Ethnopedagogy. Cheboksary, 1974.

4 Izmailov A.E. Folk pedagogy: pedagogical views of Central Asia and Kazakhstan . M., 1991

5 Kon I.S. Ethnography of childhood //Traditional forms of upbringing of children and adolescents in thc pcoplcs of East and Southeast Asia. - M.,1983.

5Kozlov V.I. Ethnos and culture/SE., No. 3., 1979.

9 Factors of popular education

Basic concepts on the topic

Nature is one of the most important factors of folk education. The naturalness of nature is generated by the naturalness of folk upbringing.

The **word** is the greatest of human spiritual treasures. Language is given to people so that they can live together and understand each other.

The **game** is a materialization of fairy tale-dreams, myths-desires, fantasies-dreams, it is a dramatization of memories of the beginning of the life journey of mankind.

Art - as a factor of upbringing testifies to the general aspiration of the people to the beautiful.

Religion is a pivotal factor in the formation of personal spirituality. The spirituality of a person is determined, of course, not only by religion.

Communication as if summarizes the effect of all previous factors - nature, play, word and deed and transfers this sum to the next group of factors - tradition, everyday life, art, religion, example-ideal.

8.1 Nature. Native word. Communication. Customs. Traditions. Art

The main factors of folk pedagogy, respectively folk education, are nature, play, word, deed, communication, tradition, everyday life, art, religion, example-ideal.

Nature is one of the most important factors of folk education. Naturalness is generated by the naturalness of folk education. Therefore, it is quite reasonable to talk about ecology as a universal concern of mankind. The statement about folk pedagogy as a pedagogy of freedom and love agrees with nature as a decisive factor of upbringing. The "Declaration of Human Rights" says: "Man is born free". Nature is the father's home, the universe and the world space. The whole traditional way of life is determined by the native nature. Its destruction is tantamount to the destruction of the ethnosphere, hence the ethnos itself.

The nature-appropriate approach in education provides a harmonious, complex approach to the formation of personality, since nature has a combined effect on human feelings, consciousness, and behavior. The principle of nature-appropriateness should be taken into account when drawing up educational programs. Much of the experience of communicating with nature spiritually enriches folk pedagogy. This experience is always national, but it never falls out of the mainstream of universal trends. Everything that is in harmony with nature should be regarded as good; that which is contrary to its development should be regarded as evil. This pedagogical principle was deeply and comprehensively substantiated by J. A. Comenius. J.J. Rousseau, I. Pestalozzi, K.D. Ushinsky, L.N. Tolstoy stood on the same positions.

Of the phenomena directly and directly related to education, the closest to nature is the game. In games are closely connected word, melody and action. An important role of children's games - in the development of children's dexterity, cleverness and agility, in addition, games are still a phenomenon and artistic and dramatic. Through games, the child was instilled with respect for the existing order of things, folk customs, teaching him to the rules of behavior. Games for children - serious activities, a kind of lessons, preparing for labor, for adult life. Play - a wonderfully diverse and rich sphere of children's activities. Together with the game in the life of children come art, beauty. The game is associated with song, dance, dance, fairy tale, riddles, shorthand, recitatives, tosses and other types of folk art. In the games most fully manifest such features of folk education, folk pedagogy, such as naturalness, continuity, mass, completeness, complexity. And what is also very important - in the process of play children are very early included in the independent education, which in this case occurs without a predetermined goal - spontaneously. The goals arise in the process of play, in connection with it, in parallel, in accordance with the result and achievements.

The educational value of folk games can hardly be overestimated, that is why a teacher should be able to use them in the educational process. Many factors should be taken into account when organizing and selecting games:

1The age of the players.

2 .A place to play games.

3 .Number of participants in the game.

4 .Availability of equipment for games.

The educator shall explain the rules of the game to the children. The educator's explanation should be brief and clear. It should be accompanied by a demonstration of individual elements or the whole game action.

The word is the greatest of human spiritual treasures. Language was given to people so that they could live together after understanding each other. In folk pedagogy, the native word stands at an unattainable height. Spirituality is associated primarily with the word, language, speech. Not without reason they say about the word: you can kill with it, you can also resurrect. Diverse in folk pedagogy verbal forms of influence on feelings, consciousness, human behavior. The verbal methods of influence on the personality are numerous and diverse: exhortation, persuasion, explanation, order, request, commission, trust, teaching, admonition, admonition, edification, wish, advice, hint, approval, gratitude, condemnation, reproach, reproach, vow, ban, prohibition, goodwill, covenant, commandment, sermon, confession, etc., and others. It is in the issue of national languages that the most acute problem has arisen today. Total discrimination of national languages has led to spiritual and moral degradation of many peoples. World, regional, official, state languages should never be studied at the expense of native languages.

Labor occupies a special place in folk pedagogy. The traditional culture of upbringing includes the idea of selfless labor's self-value. People value the unity of word and deed. Bragging is rejected.

Communication as if summarizes the effect of all previous factors - nature, play, word and deed and transfers this sum to the next group of factors - tradition, everyday life, art, religion, example-ideal.

I.V. Sukhanov consistently distinguishes the concepts of "traditions" and "customs". Customs and traditions perform two special functions common to them: to be a means of stabilizing the relations established in a given society and to reproduce these relations in the lives of new generations. But these functions, customs and traditions carry out in different ways. Customs directly through detailed prescriptions of actions in specific situations stabilize certain links of social relations and reproduce them in the life of new generations. Traditions, unlike customs, are directly addressed to the spiritual world of man, they perform their role as a means of stabilization and reproduction of social relations not directly, but through the formation of spiritual qualities required by these relations.

D.M.Ugrinovich considers custom and ritual to be the main forms of traditional folk culture. G.N.Volkov agrees with him, stating that the quantitative and qualitative analysis of customs and rituals allows us to understand not only the content, but also the system of folk education, including the processes of ethnicization and individualization of personality. Consequently, custom, rite, ritual are prescriptions for a certain style of behavior and the organization of the fulfillment of these requirements. And these requirements were selected by life itself and constantly revised by it.

E.S. Markarian substantiates the view of tradition as an integral phenomenon that includes custom, ritual, and a number of other stereotyped forms of human activity.

Customs and traditions of the people are norms and rules of behavior passed from one generation to another. Their common function is to be a means of reproduction and stabilization of relations between people, protection and preservation of their lives.

Customs differ from traditions in the detailed prescription of actions in specific situations. They transmit a standard of behavior, thus being a mechanism of cultural transmission, a mechanism of succession of generations. The most effective side of custom is the ritual form. Rites are associated with significant moments in human life, for example, the birth of a child, entry into school, marriage, etc. In the process of embodiment of emotions and ideas into external actions that form a rite, the formation and development of generally significant phenomena and attitudes to reality takes place.

Thanks to traditions, cultural experience and ways of life support are transmitted. Traditions mobilize, contribute to the unity of the people, provide moral and ethnic continuity.

Loyalty to national customs and traditions is an attitude to the history of one's people, a sense of respect for the experience of past generations, and an expression of tolerance.

The pedagogical process in ethnos is polyfunctional. There are no dysfunctions in it due to the naturalness and naturalness of pedagogical goals and means. The nature of changes in ethnos is set by tradition from within and is not arbitrary. Any ethnos keeps real and symbolic events of the past, the order and images of which are the core of collective identity. Tradition serves not only as a symbol of the continuity of the upbringing process in an ethnos, but also regulates the limits of innovation in it. The degree of development of creative function by tradition serves as a criterion of activity of ethnophores - carriers of elements of folk culture.

Art as a factor of upbringing testifies to the general aspiration of the people to the beautiful. Folk art opposes mass culture. Under the beautiful in the broad sense of the word people understood life itself in its continuous development. People saw the features of the beautiful in the phenomena of nature, family and social life, communication, labor, artistic crafts, expressive sounds (folk music), organized movements of the human body (folk dances and dances), the artistic word. At the same time, the concept of beauty included creative activity of people aimed at mastering and transforming reality according to the laws of beauty invented by the people themselves. The concept of the beautiful contained the negation of the ugly, ugly - that which contradicted the people's ideas of beauty and human dignity, which prevented the approval of the new, progressive. The people considered the sphere of manifestation and the source of the beautiful to be, first of all, everyday life, everything that constantly surrounded family members: the beauty of the home, things, clothes, jewelry.

The aesthetics of labor was understood as the friendly collective productive work of the family, community, as the beauty of the labor process and its results. The beautiful was also found in the sphere of communication and human behavior. The aesthetics of communication included the requirements of speech culture, politeness, tact, respect and reverence for elders. Folk pedagogy regarded all spheres of beauty as a source of developing in the young generation not only an understanding of the essence of beauty, the ability to appreciate it, but also the ability to create beauty.

Literature

1 Baturin A.G., Kuzina T.F. Folk pedagogy in the upbringing of preschool children. M., 1995.- P. 47-48,66-67.

2 Volkov G.I. Ethnopedagogy. - Cheboksary, 1974. - 376 c.

3 Kazakh ethnopedagogy / ost. S. Kaliev. Kaliev. - Almaty, 1996. - 22 c.

4 Kozhakhmetova K.J. Kazakh ethnopedagogy: methodology, theory, practice. Almaty: Fylym, 1998. - 316 c.

5 Kozhakhmetova K.J. Mekteptsh ulgtyk terbiye zhүyesi: theory and practice. - Almaty, 1997. - 142 б.

6 Ushinsky K.D. About nationality in public education / Ped.opis. in 6 T. / Comp. C. F. Egorov.-M.: Pedagogy, 1988, Vol. 2.-527 p.

7 Ethnic Pedagogy: A Book for Reading/Pyatin V.A., Trenev A.M., Alekseeva G.V. et al. - Astrakhan, 1995. - 276 c.

10 Spiritual and moral and education in folk civic-patriotic pedagogy.

Basic Concepts

Folk pedagogy is a system of upbringing based on the national-historical peculiarities of a particular nation, its traditions, customs, faith, and reflecting its mentality, psychological makeup and emotional and aesthetic predilections. Folk pedagogy accumulated the main pedagogical ideas of centuries-old experience of the people: cooperation in joint life activities, spiritual dedication and mercy, elevation of spiritual needs over "earthly" and much more.

Patriotism - translated from Greek means love for the Motherland, devotion to the Fatherland.

Patriotism is understood as one of the most significant, enduring values inherent in all spheres of life of society and the state, which is the most important spiritual asset of the individual. Patriotism is manifested in the active position of the individual, readiness for self-realization for the benefit of the Fatherland. Patriotism embodies respect for the Fatherland, involvement with its history, culture, achievements and values of the people.

Today patriotism is increasingly understood as the most important value that integrates not only social, but also spiritual and moral, ideological, cultural and historical, military and historical and other components.

Citizenship is an integrative characteristic of a person's personality, a concept that characterizes a person's civic and patriotic position, his value orientation, which implies responsibility for the fate of his homeland, involvement with its destiny.

Education in the broad sense is the process of human socialization, i.e. the assimilation by a person of values, attitudes, norms and patterns of behavior characteristic of a given society, social group and reproduction by a person of social ties and social experience.

Education in the narrow sense is a purposeful activity designed to form in children and young people certain socially significant personal qualities, attitudes and beliefs.

10.1 Spiritual and moral and civic-patriotic education.

Patriotism in translation from Greek means *love for the motherland, devotion to the Fatherland. "Citizenship"* is an integrative, complex characteristic of a person's personality, a concept that characterizes a person's civic and patriotic position, his value orientation, which implies responsibility for the fate of his homeland, involvement with its destiny.

Throughout the history of mankind the problem of patriotism, attitude to the Motherland, Fatherland has been the subject of constant attention of thinkers, public figures, scientists, educators. The spiritual potential of the patriotic idea is reflected in written and oral sources of the peoples of our country, all countries of the world. The very term "patriot" has been widely used since the Great French Revolution in

1789, but the historical roots of patriotism have centuries of history. Generations of Russian public figures saw the idea of patriotism as a morally organizing beginning of the life of the Russian people, understanding it as the idea of domestic unity, harmony, protection of the native land, the idea of equality of peoples, the idea of moral duty to society, the idea of responsibility for the fate of the Fatherland.

Patriotism is understood as one of the most significant, enduring values inherent in all spheres of life of society and the state, which is the most important spiritual asset of the individual. Patriotism is manifested in the active position of the individual, readiness for self-realization for the benefit of the Fatherland. Patriotism embodies respect for the Fatherland, involvement with its history, culture, achievements and values of the people.

Today patriotism is increasingly understood as the most important value that integrates not only social, but also spiritual and moral, ideological, cultural, historical, military and other components.

Our approach to the phenomenon of patriotic education is based on the definition of education as a professional pedagogical activity aimed at creating conditions for motivational and value development of a person.

The concept of the professional development program for teachers is based on the understanding of *civic and patriotic, spiritual and moral education as a socially significant spiritual and practical activity*, a priority area of work of educational institutions. Spiritually moral education is understood by us as the education of the "human in man", the development of the natural properties and qualities of man. An integral part, the basis of moral education is *civic-patriotic education*, which we understand as the education of a person with the qualities of a *patriotic citizen*, which implies respect for one's homeland, its history and culture.

In modern conditions, the most important priority is the formation of a system of patriotic education as a basis for the consolidation of society and the strengthening of the state.

The problem of correlation of patriotic, spiritual, moral and civic education is relevant for society, but at the same time it is very delicate. Spiritual education as a process of human ascent to absolute values is one of the central areas of activity of religious organizations and associations of citizens, and in this regard the activities of secular state educational institutions are closely related to the activities of religious confessions. Dialogue and search for mutual understanding between all interested parties is necessary in this sphere.

New needs of Kazakhstan society, largely conditioned by global challenges of mankind, urgently require the development of effective methods of training and professional development of pedagogical staff to organize and conduct educational work in the education system to form the spiritual world of the younger generation, a significant component of which should be the values of patriotism and citizenship.

Literature

1 ShakhanovN . The world of traditional culture

Kazakhs/Ethnographic sketches. - Almaty: Kazakhstan, 1998. - 8c.

2 Baturina G.I., Kuzina T.F. Folk pedagogy in the modern educational process. - M., 2008.

3 Kalybekov S. Theoretical and applied foundations of Kazakh folk pedagogy. - Almaty : Asma, 2005. - 320 c.

4 Suretenov S. K. Some aspects of the role of decorative and applied art in the ethno-cultural heritage of Kazakhs / Sayasat - 2000 - P.8-12c.

5 Margulan A. H.. Kazakh folk applied art. - Alma-Ata, "Oner", 1988. -volume 1 P. 109-143.

6 Kozhakhmetova K. J. Kazakh ethnopedagogy: methodology, theory, practice. - Almaty, 2008.

7 Omirbekov M. Sh Traditional Culture of Kazakhs. - Almaty", 2009. - 234c.

8 Ethnopedagogy of the peoples of Kazakhstan / Edited by G.N. Volkov, K.J. Kozhakhmetova. - Almaty, 2001 - 304 p.

9 Akhmetov M. Kazakh songs and folk traditions. - Almaty, 2011 - 241 p.

10 Pankratova V. A. Production training of tailors. - Moscow: Higher School, 2009. - 185 c.

11 Zharykbaev K.B., Kaliev S.K. History of Kazakh pedagogy and psychology. - Almaty, 2005. - 322 c.

12 Izmailov A. Folk pedagogy: pedagogical views of the peoples of Central Asia and Kazakhstan. - Moscow: Pedagogy, 2006. - 284 c.

13 Kaliev S. Pedagogical thoughts in the poetry of akyns and zhyrau XV-XIX centuries. - Almaty, 2006. - 297 c.

11 Labor education in ethnopedagogy

Basic concepts on the topic

Labor education is a multifaceted, dialectical process, as a result of which the younger generation adopts labor and social experience from the older generations and thus practically, ideologically and morally prepares for work, for the management of production and the state.

Labor is an expedient, conscious human activity aimed at satisfying the needs of the individual and society.

Psychology is a science that studies the processes of active reflection by man of objective reality in the form of sensations, perceptions, thinking, feelings and other processes and phenomena of the psyche.

Labor education in the works of classical pedagogues.

Many representatives of progressive pedagogy have paid and are paying attention to the labor education of the young generation. The connection of labor education with the social conditions of life of society and the collective is especially characteristic of the pedagogical family **A.S.Makarenko**, which is based on the formation of personality in organized socially significant work. Purposeful labor activity as one of the most important factors for the education of human character, he attached great importance.

In modern conditions, the need for knowledge of the psychological foundations of labor education has increased significantly. The content requires from the teacher a thorough psychological knowledge, the ability to take into account in his work the age characteristics of the child, the laws of formation of his personality.

One of the main ideas of **Abai Kunanbaev**'s pedagogical heritage is to ***introduce people, especially young people, to labor***. The poet and thinker believes that the standard of living of the people, its consciousness, culture, and correct relations of people among themselves depend on how hardworking people are. Labor for Abay, as well as for other Kazakh enlighteners-democrats is the source of wealth and well-being. Only labor and diligence open the way to knowledge and art, make people's centuries-old backwardness recede, change their psychology.

Labor is the **foundation of education** in every nation. Yakut pedagogues **Chiryaev K.S., Danilov D.A., Semenova A.D., Savvinov T.T., Neustroev N.D. and others** draw attention to the possibilities of labor education of the younger generation in their works. **Semenova A.D., Savvinov T.T., Neustroev N.D. and others.** The relationship of man with society, nature, with other people is carried out through labor. The **main concern of national education** - diligence, love for **people** of labor. Labor diligence is considered to be a measure of the value of personality.

Modern school should raise, educate and educate the younger generation with maximum consideration of those social conditions in which they will live and work in the new century. New opportunities are created for further growth of labor productivity in all spheres of material and spiritual production, the intellectual potential of society is increased, and the modern man is brought up in a comprehensive and harmonious way.

The **laboring family** is the engine of our society. The **core of family education** is the traditions of folk pedagogy - pedagogy of freedom and love, formation of careful attitude to labor, native culture, language, nature.

The **methodological basis of** the study are the works of the classics of Russian pedagogy Makarenko A.S., Sukhomlinsky V.A., Ushinsky K.D., works of modern teachers and psychologists on the topic of research (Ivashchenko F.I., Chernyshenko I.D., Zaretskaya I.I., Varnakova E.D., Pavlova N.P., etc.).

The unity of labor and education is achieved by the fact that man, cognizing the world by labor, creates beauty, thus affirming in himself the sense of beauty of labor, creativity, cognition.

"Labor, - wrote A.S.Makarenko, - without education, without political and public education, does not bring educational benefit, is a neutral process. You can force a person to work as much as you want, but if at the same time you will not educate politically moral, if he will not participate in public and political life, then this labor will be just a neutral process that does not give a positive result.

The **labor task** and **its solution** should in itself be so enjoyable that the child feels joy. Recognition of his work as good work should be the best reward for his labor.

In the labor activity of children A.S.Makarenko gave the greatest importance to those parallel pedagogical results (skills, abilities, knowledge, character traits and other qualities of human personality), to which this activity leads, the results of it was the maximum development and improvement of their natural forces and abilities.

Objectives of labor education:

1. **Democratization of social life**, movement towards ensuring the priority of the individual, transition to a market economy - these main realities of the present time should correspond to the content and forms of labor training of schoolchildren.

2. The **new system of relations** in work on the basis of ethnic traditions helps schoolchildren to understand study as a kind of labor activity, which is not only personal but also social in nature, requiring certain efforts, planning and purposefulness in solving the tasks set, the correct organization of the process of cognitive activity.

3. **Activity-creative task** related to the formation of moral habits, skills, creative ways of activity: the habit of bringing the work to the end, to do it well, conscientiously, to show initiative, creative approach to solving any labor problem.

4. The **task of the value aspect**, associated with the formation of value attitude to work as a way of comprehensive development of their creative abilities, a way of self-affirmation as a person who has a favorite cause, vocation, needed, useful to society and all this respected by people, collectives;

5. The **task of the behavioral aspect**, assuming the education of the desire and ability to work in a team, together with other people, to build their relationships taking into account the interests of the work team, to properly regulate their behavior in the process of collective activity, achieving success, showing the ability to self-control, self-organization, self-discipline in work.

Labor for the good of people, for the good of society is not only the basis of prosperity, but also of culture. Thus, calling people to progress, showing the way to knowledge and sciences to the youth, Abay saw the basis for solving all these issues in labor. He considered the issues of labor education as the main core of any education in general. However, labor education of a young person is carried out most successfully only *if this labor is daily connected with the labor of the majority, with the labor of the masses.*

Recognizing and emphasizing the *unity of labor education with other aspects of the development of the younger generation, the* great Kazakh enlightener noted the following main beneficial effects of social work: work awakens moral qualities, makes the inner world of man beautiful, ennobles him, makes man physically beautiful and hardy, protects him from blind obedience; inspires faith in himself and a bright future; provides a solid material position.

Literature

1 Borozdin Yu.A. Labor education in the pedagogical system of K.D. Ushinsky : Cand. ped. sciences : 13.00.01 : Kursk, 2001

2 Sukhomlinsky V. A. Izbr. ped. op. in 3 vol. M., 1979, vol. 1

3 Bure R.S., Kostelova L.D.. Development of the theory and methodology of children's education of moral qualities and relationships in pedagogy of 50-60 years.

4 Petrovsky V.A. Personality in psychology: the paradigm of subjectivity. - Rostov n/Donu, 2001

5 Kozhakhmetova K.J. Kazakh ethnopedagogy: methodology, theory, practice. - Almaty: Gylym, 1998.

6 Uzakbaeva S.A., Kozhakhmetova K.J. Concept of ethnopedagogical education of higher school students. -Almaty, 1998.

7 Uzakbaeva S.A., Kozhakhmetova K.J. Use of materials of Kazakh ethnopedagogy in the study of pedagogical disciplines. - Almaty, 1997.

8 Abilova Z.A., Kalieva K.M. Ethnopedagogy. - Almaty, 1999.

9 Izmailov A.E. Folk pedagogy: pedagogical views of the peoples of Central Asia and Kazakhstan. - M.,1991

10 Nauryzbay J.J. Ethno-cultural education. - Almaty, "Gylym", 1997.

12 Ethical and aesthetic education in folk pedagogy.

Basic Concepts

Folk pedagogy is a system of family and public education based on the national historical peculiarities of a particular nation, its traditions, customs, faith, and reflecting its mentality, psychological makeup and emotionally aesthetic predilections.

Upbringing is a specially organized, purposeful and controlled impact of the collective, educators on the educated person with the aim of forming the given qualities in him/her, carried out in educational institutions and covering the whole educational process.

Ethical education is a purposeful interaction between educators and pupils with the aim of developing in the latter the rules of good tone, the formation of a culture of behavior and relationships.

Aesthetic education is a purposeful process of forming a creative personality capable of perceiving, feeling, evaluating the beautiful and creating artistic values.

Folk education is an objective and legitimate phenomenon in the life of a particular people, the purpose of which is to ensure continuity of communication between generations, carried out in accordance with the goals of folk pedagogy

12.1 Aesthetic education

Aesthetic education is education by means of beautiful things in art, nature and the whole surrounding reality.

The main tasks of aesthetic education:

1) **development of aesthetic perception, the ability to perceive the beautiful in nature and art.** Such development is manifested in students in the awakening of aesthetic feelings, in the ability to respond to the beautiful. Faced with the beautiful, a person can admire and admire it, resent and grieve, feel a sense of love and hate, a sense of affection and disgust, a sense of joy, etc. The teacher's task is to form in students the ability to be sensitive to nature and art. In order to understand the need to know, for the emergence of pupils' ability to perceive the beautiful is necessary **aesthetic education**. This applies primarily to such types of art as painting, sculpture, music, literature;

2) **education of aesthetic taste, the ability to appreciate the beautiful.** Aesthetic taste is difficult to form, each person has his or her own aesthetic ideal. In aesthetics, beautiful is that which is able to cause favorable feelings and emotions, to bring aesthetic pleasure. The aesthetic taste of each individual person may not coincide with the aesthetic taste and ideal of another. How should a teacher behave when a student proves that music in the style of "heavy rock" gives the student aesthetic pleasure? Is it possible to summarily reject such a viewpoint? No. This is the **role of the teacher**: not so much to form certain, established, traditional ideas about the beautiful, but to teach how to correlate the aesthetic tastes of different people in different historical

periods and the aesthetic tastes of today with their own personal tastes;

3) **education of aesthetic attitude to reality, which includes active human actions to protect and defend the beautiful.** This task is not only a problem of aesthetic education, but also of moral education. Students should know the basic provisions of aesthetic behavior. The teacher should not only visually present objects of art, but also offer students to try to create such "masterpieces" themselves. This will help students learn to appreciate art and those who help develop it. The ideas of aesthetic education originated in ancient times in the times of Plato and Aristotle. The term "aesthetics" comes from the Greek - perceived by feeling. Materialist philosophers (Diderot, Chernyshevsky) believed that the object of aesthetics as a science is the beautiful. This category formed the basis of the system of aesthetic education.

D.B. Likhachev defined ***aesthetic education*** as follows: it is a purposeful process of forming a creative personality capable of perceiving, feeling, evaluating the beautiful and creating artistic values. Such a definition is relevant to a mature personality. However, even children in preschool and even early childhood are able to respond to the beautiful things in the environment, music, poetry, nature, they themselves strive to draw, sculpt, dance, compose poems.

In a brief dictionary on aesthetics: aesthetic education - a system of measures aimed at developing and improving the ability to perceive, correctly understand, appreciate and create the beautiful and sublime in life and in art.

There are many definitions of the concept of "aesthetic education", but, having considered only some of them, it is already possible to highlight the main provisions that speak about its essence.

1. It's a process of targeting

2. This is the formation of the ability to perceive and see beauty in art and life, to evaluate it.

3. The task of aesthetic education is the formation of aesthetic tastes and ideals of the individual.

4. It is the development of the ability to independently create and create beautiful things.

12.2 Ethical education

Ethical (moral) education is a systematic educational impact on the human personality, aimed at the formation of socially consistent moral qualities in a person. These include responsibility, humanity, high culture of behavior, understanding and striving to preserve universal values, development of moral beliefs and habits, high culture of interethnic relations, patriotism, stability of scientific worldview, etc. Often the concept of morality is used as a synonym of personal morality. **Morality** is a system of norms, rules and requirements set by society to the individual. Formation of morality is the translation of moral norms, rules and requirements into skills and habits. Society's morality covers a great variety of human attitudes to different spheres of life and activity: patriotic attitudes, attitudes to other peoples and their culture, attitudes to labor and products of labor, attitudes to people, attitudes to oneself. The peculiarity of moral education is that the observance of moral social norms and rules is a voluntary matter, depending on the internal motives and needs of man himself. The only punishment for their non-observance can be condemnation, disapproval on the part of society or its individual members, and here the importance for a person of these disapproval, the role of public opinion in his consciousness is important. A morally educated person treats society and public opinion as a determining factor of his behavior, as he associates himself with this society and considers himself a part of it, which obliges him to comply with socially accepted norms and rules of behavior. A person becomes morally educated only when the norms and rules of behavior dictated by society become his own views and beliefs, and the requirements imposed on the individual become the internal needs of the person. At present, the task of reviving universal values is acute. The most important of them is life. In this regard, starting from primary school age, it is necessary to educate children, taking into account their future parental responsibilities, that is, to instill understanding of human life as the greatest value, humane attitude to it, the concept of responsibility for their own children, the importance of their healthy and full growth and development, a careful attitude to their own lives. When bringing up children, it is necessary to form in them a firm conviction that any attempt on their own and other people's health and life is unacceptable. The basic human right is the right to life. Another value of humanity is freedom. A correct understanding of this definition is of great importance. Often children perceive the right to freedom as permissiveness, impunity and lack of discipline. In fact, freedom and discipline are inseparable concepts inherent in a democratic society.

Literature

1 Volkov G.N. Ethnopedagogy. 1999.

2 Nezdemkovskaya G.V. Origin and development of ethnopedagogy // "Psychology and Pedagogy", May 11, 2009.

3 Kuzmin M.N. National cultures and languages at school // Round Table. - 1998. - № 4. - C. 8-12.

4 Yasvin V.A. Expertise of school educational environment. - M., 2000. - 178 c.

5 Slobodchikov V. Educational environment: realization of educational goals in the space of culture // New values of education: cultural models of schools. - Moscow: Prosveshchenie, 1997. - C. 177-185.

6 Krylova N. Cultural models of education from the standpoint of postmodern pedagogy // New values of education: cultural models of schools. - Moscow: Prosveshchenie, 1997. - C. 185-205.

13 Ethno-pedagogical education in the family

Purpose: To analyze ethnopedagogical education in the family.

Plan

1 The concept of popular education.

2 Features of family upbringing.

3 The impact of educational tools on the process of parenting in the family.

4 Labor education in the family.

Basic concepts on the topic

1. **Folk education** is an objective and legitimate phenomenon in the life of a particular people, the purpose of which is to ensure the continuity of communication between generations, carried out in accordance with the goals of folk pedagogy.

2. Continuity is a condition for continuous development. At the same time, the very permanence in development is a concrete manifestation of the continuity between the futurc and thc past through thc prcscnt.

3. **Labor education** is a joint activity of the teacher and the pupil, aimed at the development of the pupils' general labor skills and abilities, psychological readiness for work, the formation of a responsible attitude to work and the conscious choice of profession.

4. **Family** parenting **is a** general name for the processes of parents and other family members influencing children to achieve desired outcomes.

13.1 Peculiarities of family upbringing.

Family upbringing can have both a positive influence on the development of the child's personality and character, and act as an unfavorable factor. The positive aspect of family influence on a child can be called the presence of close people who certainly love and care for him as no one else can. And, at the same time, no educational collective can potentially do as much harm in the upbringing of children as family upbringing sometimes does.

The family is a special community that plays a fundamental, long-term and important role in the upbringing of a child. A tense family environment is not conducive to the harmonious development of the child. Anxious parents often grow anxious children, ambitious parents have children suffering from an inferiority complex, intemperance of the parent forms a similar type of behavior in their child. In connection with the peculiarities of family upbringing arise the question of how to increase the positive factors of upbringing and reduce the negative ones? To do this, it is necessary to determine the intrafamily factors that influence the educational process. After all, adequate or inadequate behavior of a child depends on the conditions of upbringing in the family.

Problems and peculiarities of upbringing

Children's upbringing and the development of the personality of a little person is the achievement of mental unity, psychological connection between parents and child. Parents should not miss the educational process in relation to their own child, shifting it to the shoulders of nannies or educational institutions. This is especially true for adolescence - you should not leave a grown-up child alone with himself and his difficulties. A real problem in upbringing can become and lack of parental example. It is very important that what we want to instill in the future adult is reinforced by them. For child rearing to be effective, theory must be backed up with practice. That is, mom and dad themselves must fulfill the requirements that they make to their child.

One significant problem of upbringing is the fact that parents may disagree on their approach to raising children. This happens because each of the parents sees in children their continuation and very difficult to retreat from this idea. And on the basis of differences between the peculiarities of parenting mom and dad, there may be conflicts that adversely affect the formation of personality and character of the child. Therefore, the need to find a compromise, a common solution in approaches to education - the first task of parents. When a parent alone makes a decision, he must necessarily remember the position of the other and take into account the interests of his child. The second task is to shield the little person from discussing contradictions between parents, it is better to agree in private. Do not give the child a reason to give in to the temptation of manipulation, maneuvering between various prohibitions and permissions of parents. But in any case, making any decision concerning the upbringing of the child, parents should put in the first place not their own views and ambitions, but what will be useful and favorable for the child.

In any case, the father and mother show their love for the child in different ways. Unconditional is most often the mother's love, and the father's love is more conditional. Therefore, the ideal version of family interaction on children - when the mother in her behavior more shows purely feminine traits - gentleness, tolerance, kindness, the ability to empathize. And dad demonstrates masculine traits - vigor, will, perseverance, intelligence, self-confidence.

In communication between adults and children, it is best to adhere to the following principles of communication:

Unconditional love - acceptance of your child as he is, i.e. parents love their child not for any positive qualities or lack of bad ones, but simply for the fact that they have him, despite his behavior and misdeeds.

A significant problem in child rearing, when parents love a child more if he or she meets their expectations - learns and behaves well. But not always children's needs coincide with parental needs, and this leads to the fact that the child is kind of emotionally rejected by the family and the relationship changes for the worse. This brings insecurity to the child about himself and his actions. He does not feel the emotional security that was assumed from the moment he was born, which leads to significant difficulties. (An example of conditional love).

Sometimes a child is indifferent to his parents and may even be rejected by them. This happens in asocial families, but it can also happen in a good family, and not necessarily the parents do it on purpose and are aware of this fact.

The type of relationship formed between parents and children is the most important factor in its development. In every family there is a certain, but not always realized system of upbringing, which may be modern or backward from the realities of reality. The child-rearing system is understood as the goals of upbringing, the formulation of tasks, and the ways of influencing the child.

Kazakh people paid special attention to the upbringing of children, especially boys and girls separately.

A **child brought up by his father casts bullets** (*Ata кθpreH ots zhonar).*Our ancestors tried to bring up a boy to be hardworking, a warrior, a hunter, a singer, a dombrister, a lover of cattle, a tamer of birds (Kusbegi). Absorbed in their heart human qualities, art, labor. From the age of five they were taught the skills of craftsmanship: to look after cattle, to hunt, to chop wood, to make necessary things in everyday life from wood, from leather, from iron, etc., i.e. the art of handicraft. Fathers controlled the mastering of skills from childhood. All this is the basis of a boy's upbringing. And also, the main conditions of a boy's upbringing were: knowledge of national traditions and games (horse races, game of coup, reception of guests, singing, playing the dombra, knowledge of proverbs and sayings, respect for elders, etc.).

Kazakhs have a tradition of treating guests. The host of the house asks the guest "konak kade" (guests should tell a story or play the dombra, sing, etc.). There is another tradition "at tergeu", which begins with a greeting. The guests require children of 5-7 years old to name and enumerate 7 of their ancestors. Not knowing their ancestors was considered a shame. After that, the guests give a blessing to the children.

Three groups of a dzhigit's relatives. They are: wife's relatives (kayyn jurti), his own relatives (θ3 jurti), maternal relatives (naFashy jurti). The father is the pillar of the family. Kazakhs have proverbs: "Father is a giant tree, and leaves are his children", "A boy will grow up looking at his father, and a girl - at her mother". Ancestors taught their children oratory, ingenuity, developing mental abilities through knowledge of legends, fairy tales and proverbs.

Girls will grow up - they will decorate the village (*Czyz θcce, slot кθpкi)*

The main task of women is to bring offspring into the world and bring up children. The strength of a family largely depends on a woman. Her patience, kindness and other good qualities will benefit the family.

Respecting elders is an ancient tradition of the Kazakh people. Young people should not cross the road of elders, be polite, do not argue with elders, one should not laugh loudly in front of elders.

Kazakh women give advice to their daughters-in-law (daughter-in-law) about treating guests, caring for a child. The people say "It is not the daughter-in-law who is bad, in the house where she came".

Body Beauty. A girl should be beautiful externally and internally. Youth itself is a sign of beauty and tenderness. Kazakh girls should have a long braid. In order for the hair to grow well, Kazakh girls washed it with henna, kefir. That is why they say "Decent appearance gives birth to trust". Girls wore camisole, beshpent, borik and other national clothes. And also jewelry: earrings, bracelets, shashbau (hair ornaments). The purpose of describing beauty in folk works is to educate the young to beauty and to be beautiful.

The body is a sacrifice of the soul, the soul is a sacrifice of honor. Kazakh people attached great importance to the honor of a girl, a bride. Kazakh girls were under the care of brothers' wives.

Literature

1 Izmailov A.E. Folk pedagogy: Pedagogical views of the peoples of Central Asia and Kazakhstan, - M., Pedagogy, 1991

2 Volkov G.N. Ethnopedagogy. - Cheboksary: Chuvash Book Publishing House, 1974.

3 Kukushkin V.S. Ethnopedagogy. Moscow-Voronezh, 2002.

4 Kaliev S. K. Theoretical problems of Kazakh ethnopedagogy. - Almaty, 2004.

14 Ethno-psychological characteristics of the peoples of Kazakhstan

Basic Concepts

Psychology of peoples (ethnic psychology, ethnopsychology) - one of the branches of psychology, which considers as its subject the peculiarities of the mental makeup of different races and peoples.

A **nation** is a certain group of people characterized by the commonality of a number of features - language, culture, territory, religion, historical past, etc.

Temperament is a stable set of individual psychophysiological features of a personality related to dynamic rather than substantive aspects of activity.

Custom is an inherited stereotyped way of behavior that is reproduced in a certain society or social group and is habitual for its members.

Tradition (from Latin traditio "**tradition**", custom) is a set of ideas, rituals, habits and skills of practical and social activity, passed from generation to generation, acting as one of the regulators of social relations.

14.1 Ethnopsychological features of education of the peoples of Kazakhstan.

The term "ethnic psychology" was proposed in the second half of the 19th century by German philosophers and linguists G. Steinthal and M. Latsarus, who tried to justify the concept of ethnic psychology and formulate its tasks. Relying on the psychology of I. Herbart and interpreting the concept of "people's spirit" (by analogy with individual consciousness) from Herbartian positions, they tried to prove on the pages of the journal "Psychology of Peoples and Linguistics" founded by them in 1859 that language, religion, law, art, science, everyday life, morals, etc. receive the final explanation in the psychology of the people as a carrier of collective mind, will, feelings, character, temperament, etc. According to this understanding, all phenomena of social life represent a peculiar form of "emanation of the people's spirit". The task of psychology of peoples as a separate science is to cognize psychologically the essence of the spirit of the people, to discover the laws by which the spiritual activity of peoples proceeds.

B. Wundt criticized the intellectualism of the views of G. Steinthal and M. Latsarus and put forward an equally idealistic voluntaristic understanding of the essence and tasks of ethnic psychology. He abandoned the undefined notion of the "spirit of the whole" and gave a more realistic form to the psychology of peoples, proposing a program of empirical studies of language, myths and customs - a kind of sociology of everyday consciousness. In his version, the psychology of peoples is a descriptive science, not claiming to discover and create laws, but fixing the features of the "deep layers" of people's spiritual life. For Wundt, people's consciousness was a "creative synthesis" of individual consciousnesses, generating a qualitatively new reality found in the products of subindividual activity.

The school of psychology of peoples served as a starting point for the development of understanding psychology by W. Dilthey and E. Spranger, as well as the French sociological school. Dilthey and E. Spranger, as well as the French sociological school. Having asked the question about the nature of sociality, the psychology of peoples solved the question of the correlation between individual and social consciousness in favor of the latter. According to Steinthal, all individuals of one nation bear the imprint of the particular nature of that nation both on their bodies and on their souls. The effects of "bodily influences" on the soul cause the appearance of common socio-psychological qualities in different members of the same people, as a consequence of which they all possess the same "folk spirit". This psychological similarity of individuals is manifested in their self-consciousness. Its nature is metaphysical, and understanding it is difficult, only a description of its manifestations is possible.

Studies by scholars from different countries show that Central Asia was one of the centers where the formation of world civilization took place. At the same time, only a hundred years ago, its peoples lived mostly in conditions of patriarchal-feudal relations permeated with medieval traditions, customs, religious norms of law and judgment, and inter-tribal feuds.

Representatives of the peoples of Central Asia are endowed with:

- practical mind, rational thinking, abstract judgments and abstract concepts are not typical for them;

- weakly expressed external emotionality, restrained temperament, calmness and rationality;

- the ability to endure physical suffering, unfavorable weather and climatic conditions;

- high performance, honesty, respect for elders;

- a certain reticence in their national groups, especially during the initial period of acquaintance, communication and interaction with other people, and a wary attitude towards representatives of other nationalities.

Natural and climatic conditions were one of the factors that shaped the ethno-psychological characteristics of the peoples of Central Asia. Many of their generations, as well as other people living in hot and arid regions of the globe, have accumulated great experience in adapting to extreme climatic conditions. Traditional clothing, special housing, a centuries-old way of life and attitude to it - all this allows them to live and act successfully in familiar circumstances. Such adaptation implies a measured, unhurried life, unhurried and even sluggish work in conditions of high heat. A man works with a hoe in a measured manner, gets tired, goes to the shade, sits under a tree, drinks a cup of green tea, rests and continues his work. This is how they worked for centuries. Such traditions, preserved even today, have a determining influence on people's behavior and actions.

Most Central Asians are weak in expressing their emotions and feelings. They are mostly people of phlegmatic and sanguine temperaments. They are slower than other peoples to conceptualize life and professional tasks that arise in the process of activity.

However, when the goal is internalized, it becomes an indispensable guide to action. Representatives of these nationalities try to fulfill their official duties conscientiously. At the same time, if control over their activities is relaxed, they may indulge themselves and their fellow countrymen.

Many peculiarities of the national psychology of the indigenous peoples of the Central Asian region are explained by the peculiarity of the inherent norms and rules of social and cultural life. For example, Kazakhs, Kyrgyz, Turkmens, Karakalpaks and some Uzbeks still have strong tribal ties. Belonging to a circle of people connected by blood ties imposes great responsibilities. For example, it is considered natural to help relatives even when they are wrong, to protect them even if they have committed anti-social offenses. When one of the relatives occupies a leadership position, he or she almost always strives to create an entourage of people closest to him or her.

Kinship ties are manifested, for example, in such a national custom as returning from a long trip to bring gifts for numerous relatives. Ties of country are also strong. If the representatives of these nations find themselves outside their region, they usually stay in a close-knit group, and the latter can be formed not only on national but also on religious grounds.

Islam, which, as is well known, originated in Arabia and was planted among other peoples with great cruelty, plays a huge role in the socio-psychological formation of young people in Central Asia. The fact that Islam's doctrine is simple, its believers have few duties and its rituals are very simple has contributed to its establishment in the Central Asian region.

The peoples of Central Asia have long been characterized by respect for their elders. In addressing them, they especially observe gestures developed over the centuries that emphasize courtesy. For example, when a junior gives something to an elder, he should support his right hand with his left hand.

Representatives of Central Asian peoples take insults, including verbal insults, especially foul language, very hard. In such circumstances, they tend to get very agitated and go to conflicts. However, they appreciate very highly the even tone of other people, their high culture and calm manner of speech, as well as trust, respect, good attitude to their national traditions, customs, habits, literature and art.

The peoples of Central Asia have many distinctive features, with many external and psychological similarities. For example, the Uzbek people, who for many centuries have been mainly engaged in agriculture and trade, have developed a thrifty attitude to the earth's riches and an adaptability to hard work. The Kazakhs and Kirghiz, who from ancient times have been mainly engaged in the breeding of horses and sheep, have a deeper knowledge of all that is connected with the needs of pastoralism. As a result of broad economic ties with other peoples, the Uzbeks have developed sociability, politeness and affability. The nomadic way of life of Kazakhs and Kyrgyz, their constant stay far away from other people contributed to the formation of their considerable restraint in communication with strangers, in expressing even the most sincere and warm feelings.

Literature

1 Wundt W. Problems of psychology of peoples. - Moscow: Academic Project, 2010. - 136 c. - (Psychological technologies).

2 Yaroshevsky M.G. Psychology in the XX century. - M., 1974.

3 Pavlenko V.N., Taglin S.A. General and applied ethnopsychology. - M., 1980.

4 Krysko V.G. Ethnic Psychology. - M., 1994.

5 Ethnic psychology. A textbook.

6 Ethnopsychological dictionary. - Moscow: Moscow Psychological and Social Institute, 1999.

15 Social significance of national traditions of Kazakhstan

Purpose: To study and know the national traditions of Kazakhstan.

Plan

1 . Customs and traditions as a factor in folk education.

2 . The influence of nationality on a child's psychological characteristics.

3 .Social significance of national traditions of Kazakhstani people.

Literature

Basic Concepts.

Tradition - from the Latin "traditio" - transmission - is the elements of social and cultural heritage passed from generation to generation and preserved in certain societies, classes and social groups for a long time. Traditions are the socially defined norms of behavior, values, ideas, customs, rituals, etc. One or another tradition operates in any society and in all spheres of social life. The most widespread traditions are in religion.

Custom is a stereotypical way of behavior that is reproduced in a certain society or social group and is habitual for its members. Outdated customs are replaced by new ones in the process of historical development.

Folk pedagogy is a system of education based on the national-historical features of a particular people, its traditions, customs, faith, and reflecting its mentality, psychological makeup and emotional and aesthetic predilections.Folk pedagogy accumulated the main pedagogical ideas of centuries of experience of the people: cooperation in joint life activities, spiritual dedication and charity, the elevation of spiritual needs over "earthly" and much more.

Education in the broad sense is the process of human socialization, i.e. the assimilation by a person of values, attitudes, norms and patterns of behavior characteristic of a given society, social group and reproduction by a person of social ties and social experience.

Education in the narrow sense is a purposeful activity designed to form in children and young people certain socially significant personal qualities, attitudes and beliefs.

4 5.1Customs and traditions as a factor of folk education.

The President of the country N. Nazarbayev in his message to the people of Kazakhstan said: "The unity of domestic policy and society is connected with the unification of propaganda of national traditions and culture with political, ideological, religious, ethnic interest. The basis of national education is the native language. The ethnos that loses its language, will lose the properties of the former ethnoses. Language is the history of the people, the culture of consciousness, mood, literature".

Suitable conditions have been created in Kazakhstan for teaching in the native language and for promoting national culture to children of different nationalities. Today, 138,000 newspapers and magazines are published in German, Uzbek, Korean,

Ukrainian and Tatar. Radio and television programs are broadcast daily in several languages. The libraries of the Republic have more than 70,000 books in Korean, German, Uzbek, Uighur and Tatar. People of various nationalities work in voluntary organizations. Information on traditions, customs, national dress, music and dishes of different nationalities is disseminated through the mass media. Meetings, evenings, exhibitions and festivals are organized in schools, children's institutions and universities. Various interesting national games are organized at stadiums and sports grounds. National traditions of wedding ceremonies in the Marriage Palace and village clubs are promoted.

In 2000, the staff of the Laboratory of Ethnopedagogy and Upbringing of the Academy of Education named after I. Altynsaryn published a collection entitled "The people is an undeniable educator". I. Altynsaryn published a collection entitled "People - an undeniable educator". This collection contains traditions of family upbringing of different nationalities. Candidate's theses on ethnopedagogy of different nationalities are defended at the specialized Academic Council. All this can be called the result of propaganda of national culture and tradition of upbringing of children.

Kazakhs also have their own peculiarities in child rearing. Their roots go back to deep antiquity. For example, such a custom as taking a child out of 40 days is connected with ancient ideas that the first 40 days a child is most exposed to the influence of evil spirits, and that they can put diseases on him or replace the child. That is why a child up to 40 days was not shown to anyone except the closest people. And even the first Kazakh lullabies rather resemble conspiracies than songs, the meaning of which is to deceive evil spirits and drive them away from the baby.

Some traditions and customs of the Kazakh people are religious in nature. For example, circumcision of the foreskin of boys, or sundet. This rite originated in Arab countries, and later came to the Kazakh people together with the Muslim religion. Sundet is a very important event for any boy, as this rite joins him to the Muslim world, because the necessity of circumcision of the foreskin is mentioned in the Koran. Sundet is not an ordinary event and on this occasion a big feast was usually organized and the child was congratulated and given many gifts.

Another peculiarity of Kazakh children's upbringing is that grandparents, who were the main carriers of traditions, customs, experience and wisdom of the people, played a great role in upbringing. The first-born in the family were traditionally considered to be children of the father-in-law and mother-in-law. Children adopted in this way were traditionally favorites in the family. Folk folklore played an important role in upbringing. As soon as a child learned to speak, he was immediately taught songs, sayings and poems. Kazakh people have always valued eloquence, ability to improvise, to compose poems and songs impromptu. It is not for nothing that aytys is so popular nowadays. Children were taught a lot of things in a game form from the very young years. Everyone knows that the norms of social and economic life, values are laid down first of all in the family. Children watching the work of adults: daughters - at the crafts of their mothers, sons - at the household chores of their fathers, -

gradually they themselves were drawn to participate in the process and help. Thus, gradually acquiring life skills already by the first stage of life - mushel, by the age of 12 girls became good helpers to their mothers, and boys - young dzhigits. The girl's upbringing was initially more focused on the family, instilling in her the main family values, while the boy's education was given much more attention, as he was to become the head of the family and solve complex economic issues.

Another characteristic feature of the Kazakh people is their cohesion, mutual assistance and mutual help. The inhabitants of one aul have always been like one big family. If someone had a misfortune, neighbors and relatives tried to help. They helped "all the world". The rule for any Kazakh is never to leave his relatives and close ones in trouble, to preserve the honor and dignity of his family and clan.

In modern Kazakhstan, many customs have lost their relevance due to changes in the rhythm and way of life, as well as under the influence of historical factors. Women have become more emancipated and no longer necessarily devote themselves fully to family and children, but strive to reach career heights on a par with men. Such a custom as bride theft, although it happens, but in most cases with the consent of the bride, when, for example, the parents of the bride against the wedding. If such a fact happens without the consent of the girl, there are a number of criminal articles stipulating

the punishment depending on the incriminated article. But many customs and traditions are reviving from oblivion. These are children's customs related to childbirth and wedding customs. It has become fashionable to hold a traditional Kazakh wedding in the national wedding clothes of the bride and groom, with the observance of the main stages of the traditional wedding ceremony. Wedding clothes though have undergone changes, but in the modern dress traces elements of Kazakh ornament, colorfulness of the image as a whole. A saukele is again put on the bride's head. National crafts are revived, such as felting wool, jewelry, leatherwork, making musical instruments, etc. All this testifies to the lively interest, first of all, of the younger generation in the history of their people.

Literature

1 Izmailov A.E. Folk Pedagogy: Pedagogical

beliefs of the peoples of Central Asia and Kazakhstan. - M., 1991

2 Kazakhs (historical and ethnographic studies. Edited by Kozybaev M.K. et al. - Almaty, 1995).

3 Uzakbaeva S.A., Kozhakhmetova K.J. Use of materials of Kazakh ethnopedagogy in the study of pedagogical disciplines. - Almaty, 1996.

4 Sarsenbaev N.S. Customs, traditions and social life. - Alma-Ata, 1974.

5 Orlova A.P. Folk traditions and modern problems of upbringing.//Soviet Pedagogy, 1989, No.7. C.106-110.

6 Ovezov R. On folk traditions. // Education of schoolchildren, 1990, №3, p.33-35.

7 Aliyev A.A. Folk traditions, customs and their role in the formation of a new man. - Makhachkala, 1968.

LIST OF REFERENCES

1 θ6iΛ0βa Z. Ethnopedagogy: oku kuraly. Almaty: Kazak Elem TigΛep University 1997. - 230 б.

2 Volkov G.I. Ethnopedagogy. - Cheboksary, 1974. - 376 c.

3 Kazakh ethnopedagogy / Comp. C. Kaliev.- Almaty, 1996.22 p.

4 Kozhakhmetova K.J. Kazakh ethnopedagogy: methodology, theory, practice. Almaty: Gylym, 1998. - 316 c.

5 Kozhakhmetova K.J. Mekteptsh ultyk terbiye zhγyesi: theory and practice. - Almaty, 1997. - 142 б.

6 Ushinsky K.D. About the nationality in public education / Ped.opis: in 6 T. / Comp. C. F. Egorov. - Moscow: Pedagogy, 1988. T. 2. - 527 c.

7 Ethnic Pedagogy: A Book for Reading / Pyatin V.A., Trenev A.M., Alekseeva G.V. et al. - Astrakhan, 1995. - 276 c.

8 Anthology of pedagogical thought of Kazakhstan. / Compiled by. K.

Zharikbaev, S. Kaliev. - Almaty: Rauan, 1995. - 512 c.

9 Baltabaev M.H. Pedagogical culturology. - Almaty: RIC KAO named after I.Altynsarin, 2000. - 268 c.

10 V.S.Bezrukova. Pedagogy. Projective pedagogy: Textbook for engineering and pedagogical institutes and industrial and pedagogical technical schools. - Ekaterinburg: "Business Book", 1996. - 300 c.

11 Vinogradov G.S. Narodnaya pedagogika. - Irkutstk, 1926. - 293 c.

12 Goncharov I. New school of Russia: what to be // Education of schoolchildren. - 1997. - № 2. - C. 36-42.

13 Danilyuk A.Ya. The concept and understanding of the Russian national school // Pedagogy. - 1997. -№ 1 - C. 38-40.

14 Dneprov E.D. Educational reform and national school. // National School: state, problems, prospects / Edited by M. N. Kuzmin. - M. N. KUZMIN, 1995. C. 34-40.

15 Zhukesh K. ¥ltyts psychologiologiynyn, sipaty: Kθmekshi kural. - Almaty: Respubliki baspa kabinetu 1993. - 196 б.

16 Zhumabaev M. Tavdamaly. - Almaty: Ana tshu 1992. - 106 б.

17 Karakovsky V. A. Educational system of the school :

problems of management. - M., 1997. - 260 c.

18 Kozhakhmetova K.J., Syrymbetova L.S. Program of experimental-pedagogical work of Kazakh women's gymnasium in Ekibastuz // Information-methodical bulletin of RIPK SO "Management in Education". - 1998. - №2. - C.15-21

19 Koishibaev B. A. Pedagogical monitoring of complex education (thesaurus and

models). - Almaty, 1998 - 207 p.

20 The Concept of Education of School and Preschool Children of RK, 1995. - 28 c.

21 The concept of general secondary education: Institute of Philosophy of the National Academy of Sciences of the Republic of Kazakhstan. - Almaty, 1995. - 48 c.

22 Concept of Development of Secondary Education of RK, 1997.

23 Concept of ethno-cultural education // Kazakhstanskaya Pravda. 1996. August 07.

24 Korkyt Ata. Onyzdardyts batyrlar epics: AygapFaH E.Derbshalin. - Almaty: Kazakhstan, 1993. - 38 б.

25 Kuzmin M.N. Concept of the National School // National School: State, Problems, Prospects / Edited by M.N. Kuzmin. - M. N. KUZMIN, 1995. C.3-14.

26 Liimets H. J. Interaction of collective and personality. - Tallinn, 1982. - 75 c.

27 Manuilov Y.S. Axiomatics of environmental approach to education (experience of construction) // Methodology, theory and practice of educational systems / Edited by Novikova L.I. - M.: Research Institute of Education Theory and Pedagogy RAO, 1996. C. 47-58.

28 Moldashbaeva S. ¥lttyk terbiye - urnakka ulgn // Munalyde'r manandynynynynyn koteru zhuyessh jety/irudsch keleli M9selepi men zholdary zhθnindegi halykaralyk gylimy-prakalyk conf. 1994. - Almaty, 1994. Б. 115-117.

29 Nauryzbay J. J. Ethno-cultural education. - Almaty: FbWbiM, 1997. - 69 c.

30 Nurlanova K. World and Man. - Almaty, 1994. - 48 c.

31 Nurlanova K. Aesthetics of art culture of Kazakh people. - Almaty, 1993. - 176 c.

32 Podlasy I.P. Pedagogy. - M.: Prosveshchenie: Humanit. Izd. Center VLADOS, 1996. - 432 c.

33 Podstavko G.A. Concept of educational work. // Classroom teacher.- 1999. - № 1 - C. 12-18.

34 Roerich N. About the eternal. A book about education. - Moscow: Politizdat, 1991 - 131 p.

35 Sarsekeev B.S. Nomads of the Steppe. - Akmola, 1997. - 48 c.

36 Seydambek A. Kazak elem1. - Almaty: Sanat, 1997. - 464 б.

37 Syrymbetova L.S. Otbasynda Kazak kyzdaryn terbiyeleudep erekshelshter // Problems and ways to improve the system of teacher professional development: Abstracts of the International Scientific and Practical Conf. 1994. - Almaty, 1994. C. 121-123.

38 Theory and practice of educational systems .

L.I.Novikova: In 2 books - Moscow: ITP and MIO RAO, 1993.

39 Uzakbaeva S.A., Kozhakhmetova K .Zh. Concept ethnopedagogical education of higher school students. - Almaty: "Oner", 2008. - 20 c.

40 Management of School Development: Manual for Heads of Educational Institutions. / Edited by M. M. Potashnik and V. S. Lazarev. S. Lazarev. - Moscow: New School, 1995. - 464 c.

41 Ushinsky K.D. About the nationality in public education / Ped.opis: in 6 T. / Comp. C. F. Egorov. - Moscow: Pedagogy, 1988. T. 2. - 527 c.

42 ¥zakbaeva S.A. Tamyry terez terbiye. - Almaty: Bshm, 1995. - 232 б.

43 KhmelN . D. Pedagogical Processes general education school. -Alma-Ata: Mektep, 1984. - 134 c.

44 Khrapchenkov G.M., Khrapchenkov V.G. History of school and pedagogical thought of Kazakhstan. Textbook. - Almaty: University "Kainar", 1998. - 193 c.

45 Shilova M.I. Studying the education of schoolchildren. - M.: Pedagogika, 1982. - 137 c.

46 Shilova M.I. Socialization and education of schoolchild's personality in the pedagogical process: Study guide. - Krasnoyarsk, 1998. - 135 c.

47 Shilova M.I. To the teacher about the education of schoolchildren. - Moscow: Pedagogy, 1990. - 116 c.

48 Beisenbieva K. Ak bosaFa.- A; "Kainar" 1988 zh.

49 Kaliev S. "YΛΓΪΛΪ undsh - ul-kyzy" .-A; "Sanat" 2009 ж.

50 Kobesov A. El-Farabi. - A; "Kazakhstan" 1971ж.

51 Fabbasov S. Halyk; pedagogikasynyts nepzderyo- A; 1995 zh.

52 Duysembshova R .K. Kazak; ethnopedagogikasyn mektep programasyna yendaru. - A; "Tylym" 2010.

53 Kukushkin V.S. Ethnopedagogy. - Moscow-Voronezh, 2012.

54 Aesthetic Thought. - M., "Respublika" 2002.

Printed by Books on Demand GmbH, Norderstedt / Germany